A Great Awakening
How I Left the Church of Christ and Found Christ in His Church

Andrew Burns

An Imprint of Sulis International Press
Los Angeles | Dallas | London

GREAT AWAKENING: HOW I LEFT THE CHURCH OF CHRIST AND FOUND CHRIST IN HIS CHURCH
Copyright ©2020 by Andrew Burns. All rights reserved.

Except for brief quotations for reviews, no part of this book may be reproduced in any form or by any electronic or mechanical means, including information storage and retrieval systems, without written permission from the publisher. Email: info@sulisinternational.com.

The St. Symeon icon on the cover is used by permission courtesy of Uncut Mountain Supply. This Icon, and many others, available at www.uncutmountainsupply.com.

Unless otherwise noted, all Scripture quotations are from Revised Standard Version of the Bible, copyright © 1946, 1952, and 1971 National Council of the Churches of Christ in the United States of America. Used by permission. All rights reserved worldwide.

ISBN (print): 978-1-946849-84-7
ISBN (eBook): 978-1-946849-85-4

Published by Keledei Publications
An Imprint of Sulis International
Los Angeles | Dallas | London
www.sulisinternational.com

Contents

1. The Truth, the Whole Truth, and Nothing but the Truth...1

2. Dare We Confront the Idols?..17

3. How do you read these instructions? 37

4. Will the Real Church Members Please Stand Up?......67

5. Sir, Have You Heard the Gospel?...................................94

6. A Reason to Die, but No Reason to Live......................120

7. A Final Word? 148

For my wife Tammy, who taught me the nature of Love, Mike, my father in the flesh, Mark, my father in the Spirit, and my brothers and sisters in Christ who suspect there is more to the story.

Acknowledgments

I want to thank Tammy, my wonderful wife, for sacrificing so much of herself for this project. She is a true co-laborer and helpmeet in this life. I also need to acknowledge all those who listened to me (especially my mother) as I worked through these difficult subjects in the past few years, and thank you for fielding questions at all hours. I am blessed with a beautiful family whose love and acceptance mean so much, and I pray that you never stop chasing Christ. Specifically, I owe a debt of gratitude to the churches of Christ in West Virginia to whom I was privileged to minister for so many years. Thank you all for your instilling within me a desire for God and truth. To the faithful at St. George Greek Orthodox Church, your open arms and loving heart has made all the difference as we continue, albeit in a new direction, to follow Christ. Finally, for all those who read this manuscript at various stages of completion (Josh, Hannah, Nathan, Jordan, Brad, Dominic, and so many others) and offered their feedback and criticisms, your input has been greatly appreciated.

1.
The Truth, the Whole Truth, and Nothing but the Truth

Is it possible to know the truth but not the whole truth? When witnesses sit on the witness stand, they swear to tell the truth, the whole truth, and nothing but the truth. Are they different things? Well, Pilate, it depends on what truth is.[1] Without wading too deep into a philosophical current, there may just be a vital contrast between the truth and the whole truth, which one may illustrate in any number of ways. Consider just one.

Somewhere in your house, there is probably a jar of pennies just waiting to be counted. Who cares, right? If you counted them all, you might end up with a few bucks. That is unless your penny jar is one of those giant jugs filled to the brim with years of

---

[1] Pilate asked Jesus for the definition of Truth in John 18:38.

pocket change. However, in this time of digital transactions, physical currency can seem cumbersome and pointless, not to mention the fact that pennies cost more to produce than they are worth. It's a tough time to be a penny.

Still, it can be exciting to go through those pennies and look at the dates and become curious about all the stories these pennies might tell if they could. You may be lucky enough to find an Indian head penny or maybe even a wheat penny. On particularly lucky excursions, you may also find a steel penny from 1943. However, if you don't know the whole truth, you may pass right over one of the strangest pennies of all time — the 1943 copper penny. In the 1940s, while the war raged around the world, the US, together with its allies, pooled resources for the collective struggle. Among those highly prized resources were copper and nickel–the precious metals used to make pennies. Instead of just stopping production on the penny, in 1943, the US mint ran penny production with steel blanks instead of the usual copper-nickel alloy. Little did they know, there were still roughly 40 copper alloy blanks in the machine when the 1943 production ran, which put approximately 40 1943 copper pennies into circulation.

Now, if you didn't know the whole truth about pennies made in the 1940s, you could very easily pass over a 1943 copper penny as one of a million other virtually useless coins. If you knew the whole truth, however, you could be one of the lucky ones that find those 1 cent coins can sell for over a million dollars.

1. The Truth, the Whole Truth, and Nothing but the Truth

This is why I take the time to look at the date on every penny I come across. It just might be the one!

The truth of the matter is that the penny is worth one cent to those who don't know the whole truth. If you don't know the whole truth and if you had all 40 1943 copper pennies, you'd have 40 cents–still 60 cents short of a dollar. You would not be in error to claim these pennies are valued at 1 cent. It is important to note that knowing the whole truth does not change the reality of the truth you once accepted. Still, knowing the real value of a 1943 copper penny does not magically transform it into a million-dollar coin. Understanding the whole truth, however, adds depth and richness (no pun intended) to the truth as once accepted, allowing for a more profound appreciation of that truth. Stories like this abound in our culture. How many times have you passed over a 1943 copper penny? How many times have you passed over that $4 painting at a flea market that happened to have a first printing of the declaration of independence behind it? It's staggering to think of the treasures we've all passed over simply because we didn't know the whole truth or at least more of it.

Treasures like these would be remarkable to find, but what about the treasure of faith? Is it possible that one could be convicted by the truth but not yet understand the whole truth and thereby miss out on unfathomable riches? How would you even know? If God is infinite, as we affirm, then it seems to be true that no matter how much our faith grows or how much more we progress in the knowledge of the truth, there will always be an infinite distance yet to go. In this respect, I suppose one can never get to the whole truth, for there is no way to grasp our God and define Him in His fullness. Perhaps, more profound truth would be a better term? At any rate, can the prospect of infinite growth justify complacency? Far from it! Christians of any ilk would confess that we need to grow both in our faith and understanding of God. This is what this book is about.

My introduction to God was in the churches of Christ in rural West Virginia. For those familiar with this group, you'll notice the lower case "c" in churches; that is on purpose. The Restoration Movement (hereafter RM) churches, currently a fractured brotherhood, are hemorrhaging numbers and closing doors at a record pace, and I am one of those that walked away. For over 30 years, I called the churches of Christ my home, and for nearly 20 of those years, I was a preacher in that brotherhood. I was "located" at times and, at other times, itinerate. I held "gospel meetings," I did baptisms, I showed the Jule Miller filmstrips in people's homes. I knew the truth, but, as I studied and lived life with reflection, I came to know a more profound truth, not a truth that invalidated the first, but a truth that enriched the entire enterprise.

However, God has a way of reorienting your attention through tragedy and triumph. For me, this came in the form of the dreaded D's: death, divorce, and defeat. They all happened within a relatively short time frame and forced my hand. I came to a place in my life where the old systems and procedures of understanding foundational truths just

1. The Truth, the Whole Truth, and Nothing but the Truth

didn't seem to work anymore. I tried just to tamp it down and go on with it, but faith was starting to feel less authentic. If this story sounds familiar, then this book is in the right hands. True, it is a book about growth but it is intentionally constructed for people in the churches of Christ who have a nagging suspicion that there must be more to the story. Let's begin with a little context.

When I was a kid, my family used to take trips to the beach. All my aunts and uncles, a set of grandparents, along with my parents, rented a big house on Oak Island in North Carolina and did standard beach things for a week or two. Those were memorable times. One such memory, in particular, involved my Dad and an uncle purchasing an inflatable raft to float out in the ocean. I vividly remember a moment when, as I watched them float further and further away, I thought they had gone too far. Yet, they kept floating and floating and getting smaller and smaller in my view. I remember an instant of fear coming over me as I wondered if they understood how far away they were; did they even care?

Currents can be an alarming power only insofar as you don't realize the current in which you find yourself. If you're not careful, unchecked water currents can sweep you or your property away just as a lifestyle or cultural currents can destroy the wellbeing of anyone. Currents are everywhere in nearly all aspects of our life, moving us along often unbeknownst to many. Churches are no different. Faith traditions, or religious currents, carry us in certain directions whether we know it or not, and, like other forces, they can either lead you closer to God or further from the truth. What is important, first of all, is that we realize what current we're in, and secondly, where we might be headed at the end of your float.

Anyone who was raised in a church environment was born into a particular current or faith tradition. These traditions are formative in that they carry us along even when we are unaware of their power. Churches of Christ are no different save two interesting features; language and autonomy. As I attempt to chart the current into which I was born in order to provide some necessary context to this story, we'll have to navigate through some insider terms and ideas. In my experience, there was a sort of church of Christ language that you learned to speak with each other, and knowing the right terms to drop in the right places showed your status somehow. I will try to use generic terms, and when using one of these insider terms, please forgive me; I will try and define each of them along the way.

As I hinted at before, if you tried to put churches of Christ on a spectrum, you'd have your left-leaning groups mainly waving the flag of grace, contemporary music, and casual atmospheres in worship; people usually called them liberals. You'd also have your hard right-leaning conservative groups that took a strict view of biblical interpretation, and they normally camped out under the banner of autonomy, isolation, the necessity of head coverings, not eating in the building, and non-cooperation with other religious groups. These churches, often dubbed non-institutional churches (or anti because they were "anti"

1. The Truth, the Whole Truth, and Nothing but the Truth

everything) tended, in my estimation, to be more susceptible to divisions in the ranks. Many of these "anti" churches were small in number and were organized mainly in line with existing family structures. For example, one congregation might consist mostly of one family group or maybe two, but rarely ever were there three or more large family groups. Somewhere in between those two poles you would find other scatter groups camped out on a particular issue. For example, some congregations were known as a "one-cup" church because their communion services featured only one cup. For them, it was a central issue of faith. Finally, there were, in greater number too, more central standing congregations that took a mediating stance between liberal and anti. It is important to note that these currents of tradition, although sharing a name, never really interacted with one another on a large scale because autonomy is so highly valued. It is difficult to overestimate just how critical the autonomous issue is for many churches. Each one viewed themselves as freestanding, accountable to no one, and believed they answered only to Jesus. However, when these streams met, there seemed to always be turbulence, and it was this mixing of currents that brought me into the world. Let me explain.

My mother, and nearly all of her family, represented the traditional central position of churches of Christ in West Virginia. My father, and nearly all his family, came from the non-institutional wing. These two streams converged, creating some interesting whitewater for my formative floating. My mother, ever the peacemaker, consented to the weight of my father's conscience, and you might say my current was a center leaning conservative one. Thanks to the influence of my father and some of his close associates, the little congregation that I was raised in didn't have a kitchen, but we did have a nursery and separate classes for all age groups. This was a big deal for my father because some family believed that all people in the church should learn together in the same room at the same time and for that reason, they had no individual classes. We didn't have a fellowship hall, but we did rent the cafeteria from time to time at the local elementary school. We didn't have a church bus, but we did pick up older people from time to time and tote them around. We didn't cooperate with other religious groups in our town, and we didn't send money from the church treasury to support things like orphan homes and missionary societies. These were all critical matters of distinction for my father because he believed with all his heart that funds in the church treasury should only be used explicitly for church matters and that could never include paying someone else to do the church's work. When we met, we sang songs, no instruments, of course, we prayed, we took communion on Sundays from individual cups, we had bible classes, and we listened to sermons. For those familiar with the RM in general and the churches of Christ in particular, I bet you know exactly the congregation I'm talking about here. For those who may not be familiar with the various streams of the traditions within the churches of Christ, suffice it to say we were well on the conservative side but not ultra-conservative. We would con-

1. The Truth, the Whole Truth, and Nothing but the Truth

fess to being neither Protestant nor Catholic but simply Christians; Christians attempting to do Bible things in "Bible ways" and kept, for the most part, to ourselves.

The mixture of these two streams under the same roof was turbulent. It is important to note that I do not use the word turbulent to describe this situation because it was traumatic, far from it. I have fond memories of childhood and church experiences; I wouldn't trade them for anything. Even to this day, I can look back on the memories and smile. That current made me what I am, warts and all, and I am thankful for the religious education that came down to me through my mother and father. Rather, I use the word turbulent because, through the traditional currents of my parents and other religious teachers, I developed questions about faith, worship, and God, resulting in divergent and sometimes conflicting viewpoints. If you were to ask 50 different teachers the same question, you might get 30 different answers; doctrines were not always homogeneous unless there were the big ones. (Baptism, worship, etc.) True, my physical life was peaceful and free from distress thanks to the security provided for me by my parents, but my spiritual life was full of questions and uncertainties that sometimes kept me up at night.

I tried my best, at times, to answer these questions and share my results with fellow church members. As it turned out, I either had a knack for sharing, or maybe no one else wanted to do it, and I grew into preaching at this church regularly. That developed into preaching at other churches when they had an opening. I spent ten years of my life standing in that same pulpit preaching to the people that had formed me, demonstrating the turbulence of those intersecting views in my own spiritual life. To be sure, I was floating on a turbulent current that I wasn't always aware of, nor did I know at all times where it was going. I was taught that it led to heaven even though I wasn't so sure it did at times, and I felt sure I was charging through the frontier, calling my shots leading the way to prosperity and freedom for my little corner of Christendom. I was wrong.

I could write a million words describing the current into which I was born, the advantages it gave me as well as the scars it left, and it wouldn't ultimately matter to anyone because it is not your current; it's not your context. You were born into a cultural stream that formed you when you weren't even looking as you floated along through your formative years. One day, I woke up and looked around and said to myself, "where am I going?" "How did I get here?" "Why am I the way I am?" Perhaps that day has come in your life.

What follows in these pages is a snapshot of my journey. I'll take you through some of my experiences growing up in the churches of Christ, how those experiences shaped me, how I struggled with them, and how I ultimately resolved them. When I walked away from these congregations, I left behind many great people, wonderful friends, and scores of family members, all of whom I love dearly. Subsequently, I also write these words as an offering for these people that I left behind, hoping to expose the reasoning be-

1. The Truth, the Whole Truth, and Nothing but the Truth

hind my decision to leave. Before we get too far into that story, let me offer a few disclaimers.

First, I want to clarify what I mean when I say "churches of Christ." There is no way to answer the question, "What do the churches of Christ believe?" This is true because there is no such thing as "church of Christ" belief — it's too varied. The churches of Christ (and Churches of Christ) are spread out theologically on a spectrum, and no two are exactly alike but yet many are eerily similar. They can all trace their origins back to the RM of the 19th century led by men like Barton Stone and Alexander and Thomas Campbell. While these churches are often lumped under the heading of "Stone-Campbell Movement," they are often more likely to claim A.D. 33 as the origin date for the churches of Christ. Many church buildings with which I am familiar will have the phrase "Founded A.D. 33" chiseled on the cornerstone their church building.

Therefore, when I use the term "churches of Christ," I am most commonly referring to non-institutional churches of Christ in West Virginia primarily because that is what I am familiar with. Although these churches share a similar name, they are different than mainstream churches of Christ, and even in that strand, there is variation. I realize that these differences may not mean anything to the reader who is unaffiliated with the RM, but it's an important distinction to make for those within that tradition. It is essential to note that in the absence of a central unifying structure, an extremely high view of congregational autonomy, and geographical distance between congregations, many of the churches of Christ developed across West Virginia and the south in relative isolation from one another save for brotherhood publications like Gospel Advocate. Due to this variation, when I use the term "churches of Christ," I am only talking about the ones with which I am familiar, and I am not talking about all the churches of Christ across the globe. I know there are Churches of Christ that are healthy, focused on Christ, and encouraging one another daily to love the Triune God and their neighbor made in His image. Thanks be to God for these people. While I agree that no two congregations are exactly alike, if what I know about these churches is true, I suspect our stories will share some common ground.

I want to make a few promises upfront as I don't want to waste your time. Let me tell you what you most certainly will not find in this book. While I am one of those who have left the fellowship of the churches of Christ, I hold no ill will towards them. There was a time that I harbored feelings of anger and resentment towards the entire RM, but those times have passed. This book would read much differently had I written during those times. If you are looking for an in-depth dissertation on what's wrong with the churches of Christ, you will not find it here. If you are looking for someone to take up your cause as it relates to issues within that brotherhood, you'll waste your time reading any further. If you are looking for ammo to use in your brotherhood debates, you may want to pass this book onto someone else. To be sure, books like those exist tailored to fit any

1. The Truth, the Whole Truth, and Nothing but the Truth

theological discussion you may find yourself embroiled in from grace versus works to music in worship and the role of women in the life of the church. All those are worth studying in their place, but this is not that place for me, and I will not take up those issues here.

Additionally, I will refrain, as much as possible, from making this book a tale about personal tragedy and conquest. I do this for many reasons, not least of which is the nature of tragedy itself. Tragedy is an extremely personal thing, and what is tragic to one person may not be painful to the next, and what harrowing experiences I may or may not have endured are not the same experiences of your life. While I did experience tragedy and trauma in the churches of Christ, some people have had it worse than me. We must remember, though, that if we use tragedies alone to justify our actions, we will all go in different directions, for we all experience them differently. Therefore, I don't want to make emotional appeals, and I don't want to justify my decisions with emotional experiences. Aside from that, who am I anyway? Why would you want to read my personal story? I assure you, it's not that interesting. I do not expect you to finish this book feeling sorry for me or feeling as though you've completed an autobiography about a rather uninteresting man.

Lastly, if you are expecting an expertly constructed theological discourse, you may be disappointed. While I have finished seminary at a reputable university, and while I have written a few academic-style papers in the past, this book is not that. I am not going to interact in-depth with the history of the RM, current or past trends in RM thinking, nor with the broad spectrum of the Orthodox theology of my current context. This book will neither be a condemnation of the churches of Christ nor an apology for Orthodoxy. If you're looking for in-depth analyses of these topics, you're going to need to look elsewhere. As we move forward, I will not attempt to argue the nuances of theological matters in either tradition. Perhaps that book will come sometime, but it is not now. If that is what you're expecting, you're going to be let down. I want to reiterate here the goal of this book. It is a book about growth in Christ primarily for people in the churches of Christ who suspect there just may be more to faith than their experience has revealed.

What you will find in these pages, however, is an attempt to speak to the hearts of people in the pews in the churches of Christ or generally in any place where the souls of seekers may be as the Lord sees fit. This is not to say that folks from other faith traditions cannot find any benefit from this; who knows, maybe no one will find any profit from this book at all! In fairness, however, I don't have firsthand experience with other faith traditions. Furthermore, while I do have a multitude of experience in the churches of Christ, this does not mean that I have experienced the entire spectrum. Churches of Christ in California are different from the ones you find in any random hollow in West Virginia. As noted above, the tradition is a broad one full of variance and, at times, opposing points of view. And so, I may know on paper what it

1. The Truth, the Whole Truth, and Nothing but the Truth

means to be Catholic, Methodist, Baptist, or one of the branches of Pentecostalism, but I can't tell you how it feels to live in these traditions. If that happens to be your story, you'll have to adapt the content to your situation.

Given that, you can expect to find an honest assessment of my experiences in the churches of Christ within the constraints I've already mentioned. While I'll spare you the details of personal tragedies, I will share the theological and Scriptural issues that I wrestled with along the way, including finding my place in the world of preachers among the churches of Christ to ultimately leaving the fellowship and finding a home in the Greek Orthodox community. I hope the details of this transition from one who loved the churches of Christ to one who simply loves Jesus will be both challenging and uplifting. Even if that already describes you, I hope you find the story personally edifying and useful in some way.

Finally, to those in positions of leadership among the churches of Christ, I hope you find in these pages a well-reasoned examination of some of the difficulties facing the tradition. I wrestled, as you will read, with these issues for decades and eventually found my peace. I am not saying that the solution at which I arrived is the only solution, nor am I positing that how I reasoned through the issues is the only way to reason. I do intend to say, however, that there is no solution but Jesus, no decision but to follow him, and no hope but the resurrection. If you can lay your head down at the end of the day, confident that you know Christ more than simply knowing about Him, then you have something valuable. Remember, though, that our Lord is living. He is living, breathing, and active. The Lord Jesus leads, and we follow, there must be no stagnation.

For this reason, we must always chase Him, and though you find him in Galilee today, do not be surprised to find him in Jerusalem tomorrow. The Bible is full of stories that underscore the importance of the journey. They hold up for us the idea that to follow God means to be active and on the move, both moving through time and progressing in knowledge and maturity. The journey suggests that the truth we value today may be developed and enriched into a fresh life-changing perspective of tomorrow. In that spirit, let us take a step.

2.
Dare We Confront the Idols?

Churches of Christ are in decline both in West Virginia and around the world; the data doesn't lie. This isn't a shocking revelation. Church leaders know this, average people in the pew know this, and both wonder what must be done to rectify the situation. The trend is affecting different churches in different ways, and some are feeling the shrink worse than others. In my small section of rural West Virginia, I've seen more closed doors and dispersed congregations than I care to count. Times are tough, but these times are not unique; there is nothing new under the sun. Consider, for a moment, the time that the Kingdom of Israel and Judah faced a similar problem.

In the 8th century BCE, the Assyrian empire was growing and causing real problems for their neighbors. Around 700 to 800 years before Jesus, depending on what source you consult, the Lord sent the prophet Isaiah to minister to His people Israel as they languished under the impending threat of the Assyrian invasion. As was often the case, Israel did not listen to God, nor the voice of his prophet, and they fell to Assyria in 722 BCE. Seeing this, Isaiah turned his ministry towards Jerusalem as the Assyrian Kings set their sights on the Southern Kingdom of Judah. As the leaders of Judah began to assess the northern threat, they naturally began to find ways to protect their borders, their people, and their way of life, much like the churches are doing today. Isaiah, naturally, urged them to trust in God and his Law, but the leaders pinned their hopes on a leader of another sort, the Pharaoh of Egypt.

There are several places in Scripture where you can read this story unfold, but for my purposes, I want to focus on the section recorded in Isaiah 30. It begins with a strong warning — a woe — pronounced through Isaiah to the Lord's "rebellious children."

> *"Woe to the rebellious children," says the Lord, "who carry out a plan, but not mine; and who make a league, but not of my spirit, that they may add sin to sin; who set out to go down to Egypt, without asking for my counsel, to take refuge in the protection of Pharaoh, and to seek shelter in the shadow of Egypt!"*[2]

---

[2] Isaiah 30:1–2

2. Dare We Confront the Idols?

I was always amazed at the logical processes of the Judean leadership here. Perhaps it went something like this.

> *"Well, our brothers to the North are now scattered, and Samaria has fallen. The invaders that destroyed them are coming for us next, what should we do?"*
>
> *"There is this man who calls himself a prophet and he says we should repent and return to following the Lord because he's always helped us in the past, he'll help us again. Did he say something about not forgetting the deliverance from Egypt? What's that about?"*
>
> *"Great idea! Let's call the Pharaoh up and see if he'll help us out!"*

From our perspective, it's so hard for us to process their decisions and understand why they would seek protection from an enemy in the shelter of another enemy! But if we're honest, we do the same thing all the time; we're no different at the end of the day. We have all like sheep gone astray.[3] To that, the Lord said:

> *"Therefore shall the protection of Pharaoh turn to your shame, and the shelter in the shadow of Egypt to your humiliation. For though his officials are at Zoan and his envoys reach Hanes, everyone comes to shame*

---

[3] Isaiah 53:6

> *through a people that cannot profit them, that brings neither help nor profit, but shame and disgrace."* [4]

Imagine for a moment that the Assyrian Empire represents the force that is pushing the decline in the churches of Christ (or any tradition for that matter), and the Judean Kingdom represents the churches of Christ (or fill in the blank with whatever tradition) in today's society. The parallel, as I see it, is that as churches of Christ begin to feel the pressure of decline surround them, they may have one of three vastly different responses. First, some churches may do nothing, as many congregations have, and will surely suffer the same fate in time. The enemy does not sleep. Other churches may study the trends, the data, and seek out shelter in Egypt as they adapt to a changing world and seek to attract a new constituency. Many have traveled this road as well. If we trust what the Lord is saying through Isaiah, this won't work either. Sure, it may delay it for a while, perhaps even a generation or two, but hope in anything but the Lord will certainly come to a shameful end.

The third option, the option encouraged by Isaiah, is a treatment of the problem that, in its own way, seems illogical. When the enemy approaches, so it goes, Isaiah encourages the people to not run away from the problem neither look for refuge in other places. Instead, he instructs us to look inwardly and examine yourself. As Judah was dealing with an im-

---

[4] Isaiah 30:3–5

2. Dare We Confront the Idols?

pending threat, isn't it interesting that the Lord called Isaiah to write in a book?

> *"And now, go, write it before them on a tablet, and inscribe it in a book, that it may be for the time to come as a witness forever. For they are a rebellious people, lying sons, sons who will not hear the instruction of the Lord;* [5]

There is something personal and intimate about writing and reading the writing of another. It's for the mind what pictures are for the eye. And during this stressful time, when Isaiah could have been banging the drum on the walls of Jerusalem or staging elaborate prophetic acts as Ezekiel would in subsequent years, he writes in the language of permanence and love. As the rest of Isaiah 30 unfolds, the Lord opens his heart to Judah, accusing them of hoping in vain things and putting their trust in sources that could never help them. Judah had dug their wells in a dry land, and the Lord's fertile fields were left untapped. In all of this, however, there was hope.

> *"For thus said the Lord GOD, the Holy One of Israel, "In returning and rest you shall be saved; in quietness and in trust shall be your strength."* [6]

---

[5] Isaiah 30:8–9
[6] Isaiah 30:15

And even though they would struggle against this and seek refuge in strange places, the Lord yet promised them His mercy.

> *"Therefore the Lord waits to be gracious to you; therefore he exalts himself to show mercy to you. For the Lord is a God of justice; blessed are all those who wait for him."* [7]

What was Judah supposed to see when they turned their attention inward? If they (if we?) could only look deep into our hearts and study the motivations of our soul, what might we find? Isaiah seems to suggest that we would find the Lord searching for us, longing to be the protection from enemies that we so often seek in other places. What follows in Isaiah 30 is a beautiful example of the fidelity of the Lord to his people and the surety of his covenant with Israel. However, something keeps us from that intimacy and from embracing the covenantal love of God. Isaiah continued,

> *"Yea, O people in Zion who dwell at Jerusalem; you shall weep no more. He will surely be gracious to you at the sound of your cry; when he hears it, he will answer you. And though the Lord give you the bread of adversity and the water of affliction, yet your Teacher will not hide himself anymore, but your eyes shall see your Teacher.*

---

[7] Isaiah 30:18.

2. Dare We Confront the Idols?

And your ears shall hear a word behind you, saying, "This is the way, walk in it," when you turn to the right or when you turn to the left. Then you will defile your silver-covered graven images and your gold-plated molten images. You will scatter them as unclean things; you will say to them, "Begone!"[8]

The problem, the real crux of the issue here, is that Judah had erected idols that they trusted in and reverenced more than the living God of the covenant. The Lord was using Isaiah to get them to see that these afflictions they suffered were meant to be an eye-opening experience! They "tasted the bread of adversity" and drank from the "water of affliction" as a means to learn to hear the voice of their real "teacher." True help was always there, but they didn't see it, for they couldn't see past their idols. Therefore, the idols needed to be torn down and scattered! If Judah could only tear those false altars of hope down and cast their hearts into the treasure house of God's loyalty, then Isaiah saw fortunate times ahead for Judah.

"And he will give rain for the seed with which you sow the ground, and grain, the produce of the ground, which will be rich and plenteous. In that day your cattle will graze in large pastures; and the oxen and the asses that till the ground will eat salted

---

[8] Isaiah 30:19–22

provender, which has been winnowed with shovel and fork. And upon every lofty mountain and every high hill there will be brooks running with water, in the day of the great slaughter, when the towers fall. Moreover, the light of the moon will be as the light of the sun, and the light of the sun will be sevenfold, as the light of seven days, in the day when the Lord binds up the hurt of his people, and heals the wounds inflicted by his blow."[9]

Returning to the parallel I suggested before, what does this have to do with us? As churches continue to sense the impending invasion of reduced numbers, closing doors, and empty pews, where should they turn? If Isaiah 30 teaches us anything at all, it teaches us to face our enemies head-on by looking deep into our hearts and ridding ourselves of idols for in so doing we will see the Lord again and recognize Him as our steadfast rock. True, we probably won't find molten metal statues or figures made of wood and stone in our hearts or even in our houses or churches. This is bound to make the search more difficult. To be fair, however, it was difficult for Judah too, and they could look right at those idols, pick them up, and handle them! Even then, they still had trouble ridding themselves of such empty devotions. To what then, are we as modern people devoted? To what are our churches devoted? We might clearly say we are devoted to God, but couldn't Judah make the same

---

[9] Isaiah 30:23–26.

2. Dare We Confront the Idols?

claim too? On what, then, is our idolatry predicated? How do we even find our idols? If they are destroyed, will that reverse the trend?

As you read through these pages, you will go on a journey with me as I experienced the truth which Isaiah wrote in his book. I suspect that you will find that my experience resonates with your own. I suppose that our natural human response to uncertainty, danger, and threat is to raise idols that give us comfort, security, and a feeling of peace. When the winds of uncertainty and mystery blow, isn't it common for people to run to any number of comforts from food to drugs to assuage the feelings of uneasiness that accompany the loss of control? Consequently, these idols we raise are difficult to bring down. In many cases, they define us as people and give our life meaning and substance. It's especially difficult when we raise the idols and label them with Christian words, think about them with biblical thoughts, and impregnate them with religious hope. To tear them down, we suppose, would be to tear down religion itself or to even blaspheme the name of God. To smash them to pieces, we conclude, would be to rip the fabric of family and nation asunder. But consider this question; is it possible that we may be worshipping just such an idol? How might you know? How do you even investigate the thought that the truth we know is not the whole truth?

You could recoil at the question, shut this book, and continue down the road with me no further. Life will go on until the day it doesn't. Or, as Isaiah suggested, you could look within, try to identify any idols, and wholly repudiate them. What's the harm in looking? Perhaps you look, perhaps you question, and perhaps you seek and find that in the root of your being, it was the Lord of Heaven all along. Thanks be to God! But perhaps you search your heart and find it sold into the world of worshipping the idol of partial truth. Perhaps, upon seeing this, you tear the altars of false hope down and find true peace, security, and hope in the covenant of the Living God. Either way, it pays to look, doesn't it?

As experience with both mornings and puppies confirms, though, opening your eyes can be difficult. The light is often bright, and the rest behind closed eyes is habitually far more peaceful and comforting than the call to the day's new challenges. Spiritually speaking, it is no different. The light shines from the Lord in different ways and at different times, and, if we're not careful, we'll miss it. I suspect we frequently miss it because of the nature of the light itself. It seems to come in pieces, hints here and there really as if God is giving us breadcrumbs to entice our curiosity and turn our attention to him. If we are to connect these dots, identify our idols, and truly turn our attention heavenward, it will take serious reflection on the experiences of life and dedication to self-examination. Truly this is difficult in our modern world, but the benefits are too great to let it pass. Let me share now how it began for me.

In the reflective process, one of the most profound moments came, as they often do, in an unexpected place and time. My wife had always had a dream of traveling to Ireland to visit, as she called it, the moth-

2. Dare We Confront the Idols?

er-land. Honestly, I wasn't excited about flying over an ocean, but I agreed to go for her sake. I remember saying, "I'm going to see Ireland or Jesus, and I'm okay with either one." Once we were there, however, I was glad I consented to be part of this adventure for the experiences were all truly memorable. Ireland, as you know, has a rich history not only in the narrative of Western Civilization but also in Christian history. Accordingly, the landscape is dotted with religious points of interest like churches, monasteries, and pilgrimage sites. These sites, just as much as the natural beauty, piqued my interest.

As we were making our preparations for the trip, I attempted to find a church to visit one Sunday while we were there. Even though I had issues with my tradition, it was still my tradition and, for better or for worse, I was going to do my best to stick with it. As it turns out, churches of Christ are hard to come by in Ireland. For that matter, protestant churches are hard to come by in Ireland. As you might have guessed, many of the active churches in Ireland are either Roman Catholic or The Church of Ireland in the Anglican Communion. We never found one that matched up with our itinerary, and so we cut our losses and moved on.

Still, many churches, particularly the cathedrals or larger parish churches, were open for sightseers or pilgrims when not being used for worship. Of course, we jumped at the opportunity to go inside and take a look around. I remember being amazed at this concept because, in my experience, the person who held the key and made sure the building was locked up was usually one of the church's most valuable people. This person was on par with the person who controlled the thermostat! Our buildings were never just randomly left open for people to come in, and either look around or pray. We never lit candles, we didn't have crosses, and we didn't have stained glass. We didn't have any images in our buildings save the quaint country scene with the babbling brook affixed above so many baptisteries. Yet, there I was in a church building that looked like something out of the Middle Ages. It turns out it was. There, above the door, hung a banner encouraging townsfolk to join them next Sunday as they celebrated their 800th anniversary. This moment, as it turns out, would be a tipping point.

I sat down in a pew with the radiant glow of a stained glass masterpiece to one side of me and that banner to the other. The windows, the artwork, and even the architecture of the building said something significant to me. Here, 600 years before the RM even started, people believed in Jesus, they knew the gospel, they interpreted the Bible, and the worshipped God all without RM or even Reformation principles. It was at that moment that I knew without a doubt that Christianity was older than the American frontier. Of course, I knew that before but I never knew it experientially speaking. As the old saying goes, there is a difference between knowing about Abraham Lincoln and actually knowing him.

Of course, preachers and teachers in the RM have rebuttals for what became my great awakening. In their narrative, congregations who met in these build-

2. Dare We Confront the Idols?

ings hundreds and hundreds of years ago were in darkness and error. To hear them tell the story, Jesus founded the one true church, and sometime after the apostles died, it fell into apostasy only to be "restored" by the adherents of the Stone-Campbell following. Some teachers may even admit that there was always a remnant of faithful people worshipping according to the "pattern," but not all of them did. However, sitting there in that pew that day, that notion was shattered, and it was no longer believable. To be sure, the light was shining through the complementary hues of stained glass and for a moment, I began to see things a little differently. As it happened, I caught a glimpse of my idols.

As the dots began to connect in the following months and years, the light continued to shine and I began to see my idols with more clarity. I looked into the rooms of my heart and examined my faith in this new light, and what I saw was an emaciated representation of something that was supposed to be abundant life in Christ. The approach to the Bible that I had received had allowed me to ignore the Old Testament because, as I was taught, it was nailed to the cross anyway, and my view of church history had enabled me to neglect all the Christian history from about 100 AD till the turn of the 19th century when the Campbell's started preaching. What I was left with was an understanding of Jesus that, in essence, had no context. As I learned later, this is a real problem.

It is a problem because the blessed man of Psalm 1 shall be like a tree, but not a tree in and of itself as if the mere idea of a tree; he will be like a tree planted by the rivers of water. That is to say that we, like that tree, need a context; we need something in which to put down roots and grow. There is no such thing as a tree just being a tree without the context of land, water, and environment. Trees must grow into the soil watered by the stream that flows from the mountains that collect the rain from heaven. For some reason, though, my root system just wasn't pulling up the nutrients to feed my soul. I went to worship hungry and left hungry and angry. It was like I didn't even have root! I was being told to "grow in the grace of God," but there was nothing there to feed off of. I had missed something because all the teachers of my youth had told me that we were the restored New Testament church, and we were rooted in Scripture built on the foundation of the apostles and the prophets with Jesus himself being the chief cornerstone. If we were truly built on that, where was the continuity? Don't roots need continuity? Roots don't skip several feet and then tap into the nutrient layers, do they? Don't we have to grow into something physically present beside us?

As you continue, you'll notice a call to two reoccurring centers of reflection: context and nature. That is, what is the context of faith and what is its nature? By context, I mean, where did it come from, to what is it rooted, and where will its current lead you? By nature, I mean, is your faith a system of thought and belief that functions for you as guiding principles for living or is it the energy of life itself. More simply, is faith a group of beliefs with which we agree or is it

2. Dare We Confront the Idols?

relationship with the divine? As it turns out, how we address these issues makes all the difference when it comes to living the Christian faith with authenticity and not in dedication to idols. For me, it was coming face to face with the lack of context that led me to consider the nature of faith itself. Allow me to explain that a little more in depth.

After the Ireland trip, I had the opportunity to attend a week-long interfaith retreat where Jews, Muslims, and Christians would dwell together, free themselves from the threat of proselytization, and discuss ideas concerning the inherent dignity of humanity according to our faith traditions. Each day, a different faith tradition would take the day offering speakers, devotions, and a look at their associated worship practices. Day by day, the Christians, the Muslims, and the Jews with their Pastors, Imams, and Rabbis, took the lead and discussed the topic at hand as they understood it from their respective Holy Scriptures. Each day, at mealtime, someone offered prayers careful to address the prayer to a divine power that wouldn't be offensive. Near the end of the week, there was a discussion centered on the commonalties of all the faith traditions. The point of the whole endeavor was to see with clarity that we're not that different after all, and, to be honest, all the services were nearly the same with the names each tradition use for supreme deity interchanged. Everyone called on God using *their* speech, *their* terms, and *their* wisdom, and they believed him to answer in his (or her) own unique way. This multicultural experience had its own merit, I think, not least of which was the opportunity it afforded me to contemplate what we mean when we say "Christian faith" and what exactly is its nature. Is it a system of thought or is it a relationship with the divine?

In another way, is conversion to Christ *only* a change of mind allowing me to affirm a new set of doctrines? Concerning context, how could I be rooted in the life of the church founded by Christ and Apostles with a 1700-year gap in history? Does that not destroy the contextual system for one's roots? Yet, as my teachers said, we most certainly are rooted in that life. How can this be? That's when it hit me! The only way that the RM churches can be rooted in the faith and practice of the ancient church with the gap as large as it is, is if they understood the Christian enterprise to be a philosophy and associated dogmas to which we gave our assent. To pass these ideas on from generation to generation, one needs nothing more than to share that common philosophy. In this system, you'd need a wise teacher more than a loving savior, a book more than a cross, and a plan for salvation more than the Man who trampled down death by death. As you reflect on your understanding of things, what is most prominent in your understanding of faith? Is it Jesus the wise teacher or Jesus the loving savior? Do you see the Bible or the cross first? Do you understand the plan of salvation or the Man who made it possible? For me, I must admit, my faith was based on argument, persuasion, and the details of a "salvation plan." This, I concluded, was a philosophy of life, not a wellspring of life giving power. Faith in this construct could be transformative insofar

2. Dare We Confront the Idols?

as it was well reasoned. There remained no room for mystery or wonder.

These reflections and questions are personal, and they are signposts on a journey we make with Christ alone. As my reflection grew, I wrestled with the idea that if faith is just something that happens in your head, then God could have achieved his goals by sending a philosopher instead of his Son. Alas, he didn't; He sent his Son — a Son who is not a Son unless there is Father for even Jesus had a root system. At the end of the day, what could he rest in? Where do his roots find nourishment? Surely this was not in His teaching but rather in his Father by their bond in their Holy Spirit. I have found no evidence in the gospels at all that Jesus defined himself by his understanding of things like we had come to do in the churches of Christ. Rather, the glory of the Son was always the glory of the Father reflected in him. There was a relationship there, not just a shared doctrinal approach to life.

As the light begins to shine brighter and brighter for each of us, I think we see ways in which more and more dots connect, allowing more of the picture to become clear. As I looked ever more intently into myself I got a glimpse for the first time of the idol in my life; what unwittingly had become the object of my worship of the years. No, it wasn't made of stone or precious metals; it was, however, fashioned from the currency of my experience. I suppose that all idols are made from the currency of our experiences for, to even exist, they have to be made out of valuable things. Far from gold or silver, I recognized in these reflections that my idol may just be rightness itself, and perhaps I believed that one paid homage to this idol with morality, correct beliefs, and an arrogant ability to be confident in one's rightness against the other's wrongness. If, as Isaiah prophesied, I stood any chance at all of enjoying the days of mercy and increase, this idol, as well as any others I may discover, would have to be ground to powder and scattered to the wind. But how do you go about finding and destroying these pesky things? Maybe we shouldn't give the Jews of the Old Testament such a hard time. Maybe they're harder to get rid of than we think.

In the coming pages, I will share some of my reflections with you concerning the context and nature of faith specifically as it relates to Scripture, the church, the gospel, and the purpose of life itself. These reflections are my reflections based on my experience and yet it is my prayer that there will be a glimmer of light in them that ignites a personal reflection in your life. I hope you realize that while I appear critical of some of the doctrinal positions of the churches of Christ, I am even more so critical of myself. It is one thing to blame the current of your traditions for the way you are, and it is another thing to take ownership of the issue and do something about it. Like Isaiah suggested so many years ago, the solution starts with us as individuals. The light shines, we observe it, and we postulate what may lay behind the veil of mystery. The glimmering of light happens all the time, and so many times, we miss these moments because we fail to be observant, and we aren't we being curious. I'm scared that we are letting 1943 copper

2. Dare We Confront the Idols?

pennies of extraordinary value be spent as common one-cent pieces. We cannot be complacent; neither can we be satisfied with pat answers that seem to run against the grain of our reasoning and experience.

With that said, let's begin the journey with prayer.

> *"Our Holy Father, the Holy One of Israel, the fountain of mercy, of grace, and of love for us your creation, shine within our hearts the glorious light of your loving face. Show us our idols and give us the strength to tear them down. Enlighten the darkness in our hearts, still the raging storms in our soul, and fill us with the peace that passes all understanding. May we always hunger for You, may we not rest till we rest in the blessed fellowship of Your nature, our God, our Father together with your Son and your Holy Spirit for you are blessed both now and forever and to the ages of ages, Amen."*

3.
How do you read these instructions?

As I was so frequently taught, if one is to be pleasing to God, they must "speak where the Bible speaks and be silent where the Bible is silent." For most in the churches of Christ, questions of faith and practice begin and end in Scripture. As I've mentioned before, there were many moments that caused me to look intently at my faith and practice and pose some serious questions. Some of these were external factors, separate from the current of the formative stream of the churches of Christ. These external factors, as important as they are, are unimportant for our purposes here. Experiencing tragedy and trauma is a highly personal event and, while I don't mind sharing my tale, it's irrelevant for your story and how you wrestle with your faith. We all have our tragedies with which we struggle. In that spirit, here, I want to look closely at some internal factors relative to the stream itself that, upon deeper examination, caused me to raise the questions I did and offer some brief reflections.

I was always a curious kid, or so I was told. Like many kids, one of the go-to questions that I kept in the holster was, "why?" To me, and probably to most curious people, learning the why that lay behind things filled me with awe and satisfaction that rivaled no other sort of story. One of my favorite programs to listen to was Paul Harvey's Rest of the Story for this very reason. He gave me the backstory. He let me look under the hood and understand the motivation behind the stories of our day and legends of our past. Perhaps this is what attracts me to the penny story from before. When it comes to movies, my favorite ones are often prequels where, you guessed it, I get to learn all the backstories for the first release and witness the arena in which the characters I first loved were formed. When it came to the business of "doing church," I was no different. I often bounced questions of my both my parents about baptism, worship, preaching, biblical interpretation, and the words in prayers. I was in High School when I first discovered this revolutionary thing called the biblical commentary. I was floored! I just had to know why we did the things we did!

I remember one conversation in particular that I had with my father, who told me about the evil ways of the Pope of Rome. I was told that he was the boss of all the Catholics in the world, and they had to do whatever he said whenever he said it. But we, not being Catholic, had our boss – the B.I.B.L.E – yes, that's

3. How do you read these instructions?

the book for me! We stand alone on the Word of God, the B.I.B.L.E! There was my answer! The Bible told us what to do! It was an amazing thought that you could go to the Bible and coax out justification and reason for all your faith-based undertakings.

When someone introduced the topic of biblical interpretation, it almost certainly triggered the use of *the* biblical illustration par excellence. I don't remember who first used the illustration with me, but it stuck, and I, in turn, used it for many years in my preaching. It went something like this. Suppose you're on a desert island, and you know nothing of religion, faith, or the church; you're a total amnesiac. One day, a Bible washes up on shore, and you pick it up and read it. From simply reading it and following obvious rules of interpretation, you could establish the pattern for the New Testament church, and it would look exactly like what we were doing as churches of Christ in the modern time. Such a castaway couldn't claim to make a new church; this poor soul was said to have merely restored it. Sometimes the story was prefaced with a similar story about baseball and discovering a baseball rule book in some dystopian world. If they brought the game back by following a once lost rule book, then they should be restorationists and not reformers; hence our label as RM churches. Our job was to cut the fluff and preach the stuff. Speak where the Bible speaks and be silent everywhere else, or for some preachers, do Bible things in Bible ways. If we could only do what the Apostles did, then we'll get what they got! It seemed simple enough.

This time in my life was filled with a flurry of study, particularly as I was exposed to other religious traditions. Why didn't my friends at the local Baptist church follow the same simple pattern? For example, why did we go to church on Sunday and not Saturday like the Adventist kids at school? Well, I learned there's a bible verse for that. Why did we sing and not have instruments like many of my friends did? There was a verse for that too. Why was the name on the church sign church of Christ (with a little c) and not something else like Methodist or Lutheran? There was a verse for that too! This verse, Romans 16:16, was sometimes put on Sunday bulletins and even license plates to let the world know that "the churches of Christ salute you!" I was told by my faithful teachers in this period that there was a pattern for New Testament Christianity, and being faithful to God meant following the pattern. But how were you supposed to find the pattern?

As I continued to study more about this pattern for New Testament Christianity, my curious nature ramped up a little more. Why was the pattern the way it was? Why did the pattern include five acts of worship to be carried out on Sundays only?[10] Why could I not call the preacher our Pastor like my friends did? The questions seemed to multiply geo-

---

[10] For those unfamiliar, for a church service to be a scriptural church service it had to include 5 distinct acts of worship: Singing, Praying, Collection (offering of money), A Sermon, and the Lord's Supper. Since the Lord's Supper could only be done on Sunday's, corporate worship was confined only to the worship hours on Sunday. Any other meeting was for Bible Study only.

3. How do you read these instructions?

metrically. One answer would change the details of another question I had already settled on, and I often found myself going back to the beginning again and again. I was told that the pattern of the New Testament Church was founded on Biblical Authority and that for us to do anything in the realm of faith, we needed to have biblical authority for it. Naturally, I wondered, "how do you find Biblical Authority?"

I think I was asking too many questions at this point because instead of giving me direct answers, people began to throw books at me. Now you should know, I hated reading. I never read any book in school that I was assigned, and I took great pride in that. My mother, who was involved with the State Reading Council, did not share my pleasure. Reading repulsed me. But these books? Commentaries? Sermon compilations? I could read them all day! They were the marrow in the bone I was chewing on! They told me how to find the biblical pattern! If you're not familiar with how many RM churches find biblical authority, or the pattern, it has to do with the locating biblical Commands, then approved Examples, and finally making Necessary Inferences after studying the first two; this is CENI for short. I'll provide a quick example of how this acronym works in practice.

One of the main acts of Sunday worship was the taking of the Lord's Supper. We did this because we were commanded to do as much.[11] Not much argument there really, this one is cut and dry. The early

---

11   Mark 14:22 or 1 Cor. 11:35 for example.

church, however, seemed to be following this command on Sundays.[12] This was the example. So, since the early church "broke bread" on the first day of the week, then that is what we ought to be doing to for that is what the Bible is "telling" me to do. Easy enough, right? The necessary inference, however, proved to be the burr in the saddle for many. One would have to make the inference that since every week had the first day, then we must take the Lord's Supper every first day of every week. In this way, commands, examples, and necessary inferences worked together to sketch out the pattern for New Testament worship and living. To do anything contrary to that pattern would be to live in open rebellion to biblical authority and God himself.

To be sure, however, biblical interpretation is just not that cut and dry. There are a host of issues that can, and should, be raised about the conclusions and ideas presented to us for acceptance. As I grew, I became bolder and more insistent that my questions be addressed honestly and intellectually, and I became increasingly repulsed by pat answers and emotional appeals. I know that people within the tradition are aware of these inconsistencies, and some people spend not a little time defending a particular approach. Still, space does not permit the listing every single question or objection for it would fill a volume in and of itself. Instead, I'll share just a few simple

---

12 Acts 2 or Acts 20:7 would work here; note the phrase "broke bread" or "breaking bread." This was taken as a synonym for the communion service.

3. How do you read these instructions?

examples of those unresolved issues that should be an indication that something is missing.

As mentioned above, the Lord's Supper was observed every Sunday. But in the series of biblical texts used to justify and support this practice, we read the text where Jesus instituted this meal on a Thursday. Is that not an example of taking the Lord's Supper on a Thursday? So, should we take communion on Thursday or Sunday? How do you determine which day takes precedence? Or is the text suggesting that the day is irrelevant? The early church met daily; why did we not meet daily? Is this not an approved example of first century worship? They met in an upper room; why didn't we? Given the Apostolic example, shouldn't we all have upper rooms in which to meet? They met in people's houses and didn't seem to own property with pews and songbooks and a pulpit; why did we? Are these not all approved examples? They sang psalms, hymns, and spiritual songs, but we rarely sang a psalm. Shouldn't we? It's in the Bible! Pianos were deemed an addition because it wasn't "scriptural," but we allowed PowerPoint presentations, baptisteries, and a host of other things because they were thought to be "aids," not "additions." How do you even tell the difference? I could go on, I mean, Jesus washed feet, but we didn't. They went out two by two; we didn't. They went on missionary trips, healed the sick, fed the hungry, ministered to the poor, and welcomed the sinner. We did none of those things. I often wondered, "Have we focused so much on the pattern that we forgot the purpose?" Maybe you've struggled with such inconsistencies as these? What are you supposed to do?

As it is, trying to get at these nagging inconsistences is difficult because of another question which no one seems to agree on; what do you do with biblical silence? When the song is finished, there is silence. It's finished, right? However, when a conversation goes silent, that discussion may in fact be far from over. Many a spouse on the receiving end of the silent treatment will testify to that reality. So, when you hear the silence, is the story over, or is there more to it? When the Bible is silent, does that bind us or liberate us? Paul Harvey would famously say at the end of his show, "and now you know the rest of the story." This line was only uttered after he had peeled away the layers of mystique and displayed the once covered underbelly of the day's narrative. I liked this part because he picked up the story again, where once there was only a silent curiosity. Yet, when you have a silent curiosity about a biblical text, how do you determine the rest of the story? True, applying the rules labeled by CENI simply don't answer all the questions; in fact, they raise even more questions.

Here, I think, lies the source of so much strife and discord among the churches of Christ specifically in West Virginia but perhaps on a much larger scale. To be fair, this entire interpretational issue, the Regulative Principle (hereafter RP), is a point of contention for many churches whose traditions stream from the Reformation. The issue is silence itself and their inability to determine how we will treat it. Who can blame them really, do any of us know what to do with

3. How do you read these instructions?

the silence? Do we not leave the TV on just for background noise? Silence can be deafening.

It is worth spending a moment on the RP and its cousin the Normative Principle; that is, do the Scriptures regulate or set forth the norm? You can't simply go the Scripture to answer that question as it has to do with the way you read Scripture in the first place. It's as if you need to have that question sorted before you even begin. Historically, churches of Christ are not the only traditions embroiled in this puzzle. The churches of Christ having their roots in Scottish Presbyterianism are quietly shaped in the background by the Westminster Confession of faith. The RP, "set forth in the Westminster Confession...forbids worship "not prescribed in the Holy Scripture" (XXI, 1). On this principle, "whatever Scripture does not prescribe is forbidden."[13] This Presbyterian context is the traditional current in which the RM founders, Barton Stone and Alexander Campbell, were formed. It makes sense that they would carry some of that baggage forward as the movement which bears their name (the Stone-Campbell movement) took shape. This principle, as opposed to the Normative Principle, takes a view of silence as something that forbids. However, in the normative camp, people see silence as something that is permissive because they believe the Scriptures to be the norm, not the regulator. It's easy to see how these two approaches to silence lead to divergent views of worship, and Christian practice

---

13 Robert Webber, *The Ministries of Christian Worship*, vol. 7, 1st ed., The Complete Library of Christian Worship (Nashville, TN: Star Song Pub. Group, 1994), 61.

for it can't be both ways at the same time. "Adherents of the regulative principle ask, "Where does Scripture command or sanction a particular practice or form?" Those who hold to the normative principle ask, "Where does Scripture forbid it?"[14] So which is it; does silence forbid or allow?

I'll go back to the Lord's Supper example from before. Following the rules of CENI, the argument went something like this. We have a command to do it, the early Christians did it on the first day of the week, and we must infer that it was every first day because every week has the first day. As it turns out, this part was only part of the issue. Granted, not all reasonable people would call the inference mentioned above "necessary," but still, this line of thinking was not what raised the eyebrows in my experience. The camel's back-breaking straw was always tied to questions about silence. Does this line of thinking exclude all other approaches, or, since all other approaches are not mentioned, are they thereby allowed?

As always, there are two sides to the story. Biblical silence on a topic either forbids something or is a license to do something. Everyone had an opinion. Every church had an opinion. But, since we valued autonomy so highly, there was never any voice of reason to call all the congregations down and let cooler heads prevail. Again, there were many go-to illustrations to demonstrate each side's understanding of things. My circle of churchgoers most frequently used

---

[14] Alan Cairns, *Dictionary of Theological Terms* (Belfast; Greenville, SC: Ambassador Emerald International, 2002), 310.

3. How do you read these instructions?

the example of a shopping list or a cake recipe. It goes something like this. Suppose your grandmother's cake recipe calls for two eggs, 2 cups of flour, 2 cups of sugar, and 1 cup of milk. And you, in your infinite wisdom, decide to change it to 3 eggs and 2 cups of milk, you might get a cake, but it wouldn't be your grandmother's cake because you changed the pattern. To have your grandmother's cake, you must follow the recipe (read pattern), and if the recipe is silent about something, you should be too. Some preachers would add here that if your grandmother's recipe for cake didn't mention adding horseradish, that surely would not be a license to add it! Those who were in favor of silence being liberating told a different story. Sometimes they would say, "Instrumental music is okay because the Bible does say you can't have it!" Still, others would retort, "it's about intention! If I make grandma's cake and it doesn't call for vanilla, but everyone in my family likes vanilla, she wouldn't care. She would tell us to add it and make us all happy! If you knew grandma, you'd agree!" To be fair, both sides of the argument make good points.

In my view, the silence (really the RP) issue was *the* issue for churches of Christ, and many of them, in my experience, never recognized that. The two opposing camps settled into their views while hurling labels like liberals and antis at the other camps. It wasn't productive. The conservative branches heaped speakers, books, and publishing houses to themselves, and the liberal branches did the same. The conservative branches urged people to follow the pattern of New Testament Christianity while the more liberal branches urged people to dwell in grace, freedom, and love. To hear their debate and to read their rhetoric, you would think they approached the bible in two different ways, and for all intents and purposes, they did.

Interestingly, both camps used the same method of biblical interpretation – they just never agreed on the role of silence. Subsequently, the current split and people began to float in different directions. When rivers split like this, it's called river bifurcation. Sometimes it happens naturally, and other times man instigates it for some environmental benefit. Occasionally the currents come back together, but often they don't. When they do come back together, they create an island in the river. I'm afraid that many good people are stranded on that island in the RM stream wondering what's going on and longing for something more. Remarkably, as is the case of the Hase River in Germany, sometimes a current flows through land that it just can't navigate and splits never to return flowing into separate drainage basins. I think this is a good image of what has happened and what is happening in the churches of Christ. Problems with biblical interpretation and bickering of what to make of biblical silence created a bifurcated stream, and downriver from that, we have some floating on one branch arguing with those floating on the other branch about whose branch is the best and the correct branch. And then there are folks like me who look up from the drift and say, "you know, we used to be one river, one stream, and one current – shouldn't *that* one be the ideal one?"

3. How do you read these instructions?

What if we've missed the treasure because we were arguing about the treasure chest? What if the question is not about regulative principle versus normative principle at all? What if instead of failing to be satisfied with all these imperfect answers, we started asking better questions? Instead of asking, "How do I interpret the Bible?" what if we paused and asked, what even is the Bible? Let me illustrate this issue by showing how one's method of biblical interpretation cannot address the nature of the Bible itself.

Let's take a look at the CENI method a little closer. It should be noted that in more recent times, I think, as a reaction to the push against CENI, teachers within the tradition have begun to use the phrase "tell, show, and imply" (TSI) as a replacement. Doy Moyer, in his 2016 book *Mind Your King*, gives what I consider to be the standard introduction to this method of biblical interpretation. In defense of the process, He writes,

> *"[W]hen we want to make our will known, how do we do it? Everyone who communicates in some fashion will do so by one of these three ways: 1) We tell someone; 2) We show someone; 3) We imply something we expect people to get. This is the more basic version of CENI. When people disparage CENI, they may not have thought this point through. Attacking CENI, as if that is inherently the problem, is attacking the foundation of communication, and it won't logically stand..."[T]ell show imply" is a logically*

> *necessary process if any communication will take place. Again, it is the way we communicate anything."*[15]

I've heard many sermons and lectures and read many books about how to coax biblical authority out of the Scriptures, and Moyer's, while not technical, is a good as any. What I like about Moyer's approach (besides the fact that we're distantly related) is how accurately he reduces the issue to its underlying principles and difficulties.

As I wrote above, the inconsistencies with the CENI approach initially opened my eyes to the idea that something was wrong. There are some writers and apologists for the CENI approach that take those objections and inconsistencies one by one and justify the traditional interpretation or perhaps even new interpretations in some cases. In my opinion, this only further clouds the waters. But Moyer's approach sidesteps the issue completely. Right at the beginning, he admits that abuses of the CENI method of reading Scripture should be handled on a case by case basis and that abuses are not a cause for dismissing the entire process. On this point, he is right. It doesn't make sense to toss out all automobile transportation just because a few people drive too fast. Inconsistent applications of the CENI method are not the issue with the CENI method at all. Too many people, in my opinion, get lost in that.

---

[15] Doy Moyer, *Mind Your King*. (Birmingham AL: Moyer Press, 2016). 179-180.

3. How do you read these instructions?

Moyer, sidestepping the red herrings, continues by trying to make the case that CENI, or TSI, is the foundation of all systems of biblical interpretation. This is an important first step because, as some within the tradition figure, interpretational approaches, or hermeneutics, can be seen as human made intrusions into the divine Scripture and, therefore, should not be insisted upon being non-essential. Moyer, yet again, avoids the trap of trying to show that CENI is a hermeneutical system. Still, CENI versus any other hermeneutic is not the issue. Moyer's point, and I think he's right here, is that TSI is foundational to all the hermeneutical systems, and to tear down the TSI method is to fundamentally undermine all hermeneutics. He adds,

> "We are speaking of the bare bones of what we work with when we do interpret. Instead of criticizing the communication process, let's recognize it for what it is and then deal with how we should properly understand the statements, examples, and implications."[16]

Thanks to Moyer's approach, we can set aside issues that stem from both CENI's abuses and inconsistencies. Surely, those issues abound and are worth talking about at some point, but they are not in and of themselves the real issue. Additionally, we should look past the discussion of CENI as a system related to other hermeneutical systems for, again, CENI being

---

16   Ibid, 181.

the preeminent interpretational approach among all the others is not the issue. I think Moyer is right, so far, on all these issues. CENI, or TSI, should not be tossed out because of its abuses or its validity as a system for it exists, in some form, in all systems. Bypassing those, then, let's get to the real issue.

Moyer, along with traditional churches of Christ, believes the traditional hermeneutical system to be the correct way to understand communication from God in Scripture, for it is the way all communication works. Here is the sticking point. They are right only insofar as Scripture is in fact God's communication to man. Nearly all *sola scriptura* based hermeneutics begin with this premise. If, however, Scripture is something else besides God's communication to man, then those who approach Scripture have fundamentally missed the point altogether, for they begin on a false premise. I am aware that to even suggest such a reality is to challenge the very foundation of faith for many people. I realize that your faith may "stand alone of the word of God, the B.I.B.L.E," and the seriousness of what I am suggesting is not lost of me. However, hear me out.

One of the first things students of biblical interpretation are taught is the importance of context; context determines the meaning of everything. Even the most basic unit of language and communication, the word, must have context before it has any meaning at all. Take, for example, the word run. Could you say for sure what it means? It could be read as a verb indicating that you're moving on foot at a pace faster than a walk. Or, it could mean that you are vying for

3. How do you read these instructions?

a political office. It's still a verb in this case, but to run for a political office carries no association with speed. Still, you could use the word run to describe the way a river moves through the countryside even though the river doesn't have legs. Could this have something to do with why people run a bath? Still, all those could be the wrong understanding, and we could interpret run as the dried paint on the wall that someone failed to clean up before it dried. Without context, words have no definite meaning; rather, they only have a semantic range of meanings.

The word run is in 1 Corinthians 9:24. If you take the word "run" in and of itself separate and apart from all the other words in verse 24, you are left with a communication problem, for there is no way to determine what the word run means without the other words. However, if we take the rest of the words in the verse, we can be sure that we know what the word run means in that context.

> *"Do you not know that in a race all the runners compete, but only one receives the prize? So run that you may obtain it."*[17]

It's clear that St. Paul is using the word run in the context of a race. Because of the context, we can know that Paul is using "run" the same way you might use it to describe athletic contests. But context is not finished here. Is Paul acting here as a coach? Is he en-

---

17   1 Cor. 9:24.

couraging people to achieve high levels of performance in some Olympic style events? If we take this verse all by itself, we have no way of knowing. To be sure, verses, like words, need context.

> *"Do you not know that in a race all the runners compete, but only one receives the prize? So run that you may obtain it. Every athlete exercises self-control in all things. They do it to receive a perishable wreath, but we an imperishable. Well, I do not run aimlessly, I do not box as one beating the air; but I pommel my body and subdue it, lest after preaching to others I myself should be disqualified."*[18]

I hope you see the pattern developing here. We needed the structure of the sentence to accurately define the word, and we needed the structure of the paragraph to precisely define the sentence. Looking at the context allows us to see that St. Paul is not a track coach, but he is using the analogy to describe the sort of determination and focus that we need in our Christian "race." There is, however, a greater problem looming here. When we get to a point where something makes sense to us, we begin to wrestle with the temptation to cut the communication off, assuming that we've got the message. I teach High School Mathematics, believe me, people do this all the time. It's so tempting to move on in the interest of time

---

18 1 Cor. 9:24–27.

3. How do you read these instructions?

once we think we've heard what is being said. So have we heard all of what Paul was saying, or did we stop short?

Sentences are to words as chapters are to paragraphs. The word "run" is contextualized by the surrounding words, those words are contextualized by the surrounding sentences, and those sentences are contextualized by the surrounding paragraphs, or in most bibles, chapters. If you want to understand the communication of St. Paul in 1 Cor. 9:24, we have to admit that it is part of a larger structure that eventually runs from the first verse of the book to the last. In this way, to understand St. Paul's communication, one needs to understand the entire book. Still, it doesn't end there.

What was the context of St. Paul's authorship? There must have been some reason that Paul wrote the book in the first place, is that not necessary to understand the communication? Scholars call this authorial intent and, while it can be difficult to ascertain, is it not vital to the meaning? Might we understand more of Paul's teaching represented in 1 Corinthians by studying his thinking in other letters? What about his life? If we want to contextualize 1 Corinthians along with his other letters, shouldn't we attempt to place them into the structure of the book of Acts? Surely this would provide some historical context to the events that led to Paul's writing in the first place.

In my experience with the churches of Christ, I was either a part of or led too many studies of 1 Corinthians to count. To be fair, nearly all of those studies did pay attention to the context as I've described it thus far, even going as far as to locate a potential context for the writing of the book within the book of Acts. However, there is one element of context that I always missed, and it boils down to the issue with CENI and biblical interpretation in general.

Not only is there an authorship context, but there is also a readership context. Paul wrote a letter to the church at Corinth to address issues in Corinth, and he most likely did not entitle it "1 Corinthians" when it left his desk. Accordingly, after the church at Corinth read the letter and digested its contents, there had to be another person or persons who realized a need to preserve the letter for posterity. Unless one is willing to affirm that the Bible fell out of the sky one day, then we will have to affirm that there was an intentional effort to save these letters and compile them in some fashion. Even today, there are many extant copies and fragments of Paul's Corinthian letter. Because of its inherent value to the churches, we have Paul's 1st and 2nd letter to the Corinthians, but not a 3rd or a 4th. We have a letter to the Colossians but not Laodiceans.[19]

The same could be said about all the books of the Bible, along with their respective canonical ordering. For example, the entire New Testament would carry a different tone if the Revelation letter came first instead of Matthew. Yet, some actual historical people put that book last and four gospels, rather than one harmony (which existed as early as the 2nd century –

---

19   Col. 4:16

3. How do you read these instructions?

Tatian's Diatessaron), first, followed by Acts, then Paul's letter, then the general epistles with the Revelation at the end. Someone, or ones, consciously put Paul's letters in order according to length, followed by his (?) letter to the Hebrews. You see, the context I missed all those years ago was the larger context of the formation of the canon of Scripture. Again, unless you're willing to affirm that the Bible fell out of the sky in its current form, then we must admit that even the Bible has a context that is its interpretational tool just like the rest of the words in the sentence taken as a whole define the word "run."

There is a fallacy in thinking that we can "stand alone on the word of God, the B.I.B.L.E" as THE communication from God in the form of divine Scripture because if it weren't for the context in which Scripture developed ultimately giving us the Bible, we wouldn't even have a Bible in which to believe. It was the context of Scriptural development that initially and preeminently confirmed the writing as an authentic witness to the truth as they understood it in actuality. Saying that we can stand alone on the Bible and nothing else is akin to saying I can define a word without the other words in the sentence. It is well beyond the scope of this short book to illustrate the entire process of the formation of the canon of Scripture. Fortunately, many great scholars and theologians have written on this topic and have come to some sort of consensus. One such scholar, Lee Martin McDonald, concludes an essay with this observation: (emphasis mine):

> In summary, it was important to the church that its writings were produced by apostles or those close to them, e.g., Mark and Luke. It was also important, especially in the second to the fourth centuries, that these **writings conform to the church's broad core of beliefs**. The significance of the New Testament writings to the churches is shown by their widespread use in the life, teaching, and worship of those churches, and such use also contributed to their canonization. The end product of the long and complex canonization process was an authoritative and inspired instrument that continued to be useful in the ministry and worship of a changing church. That instrument clarified the church's essential identity and mission as a community of Christ.[20]

If you stop and think about what McDonald is saying here, it makes real sense. He's saying that of all the writings floating around in the first few hundred years of church history, the ones that eventually became our Bible were selected because they "conformed to the church's broad core of beliefs." That is to say, faith and practice not only provided the impetus for Biblical authors to write the words they did, but it was also *that same faith and practice* that eventu-

---

20 Lee M. McDonald, "Identifying Scripture and Canon in the Early Church: The Criteria Question,", *The Canon Debate*. Lee M. McDonald, and James Sanders, Eds. (Peabody, MA: Hendrickson Publishers, 2008), 439.

3. How do you read these instructions?

ally informed which books were Scripture and which books were to be disregarded. In other words, not only did Christian faith *precede* the New Testament writings, they *established* them. What we read about in the Bible is not so much the *source* of Christian faith as it is a *witness* to the original faith.

Using the CENI approach, or any other approach for that matter, begins with a fundamental flaw presupposing that faith stems from Scripture when in the actual course of history, it happened the other way around. I realize this is a tough pill to swallow. When I came to this realization, it rocked me particularly because I always thought we stood on Scriptural authority, and to have that foundation called into question is, in essence, to question everything. Yet, interestingly, the Bible *never* claims that *it alone* is the underpinning and authority for our faith and practice. Consider a few passages.

First, Jesus reserves the foundational and authoritative claim for himself in Matthew 28:18 as he said, "All authority in heaven and on earth has been given to me." That the first Christians believed this to be so is demonstrated in other New Testament writings such as Ephesians 5:23 and Colossians 1:18, where Christ is said to be the head of the church. Naturally, the head is a position of authority, and the rest of the members are bound to follow the direction that comes from the head. In 1 Corinthians 3:11, Paul likens Jesus to the foundation and, along with him as the chief cornerstone, Paul adds that the foundation includes the Apostles and the Prophets. Nowhere do we see that our foundational and authoritative system relegated to a body of Scripture. Perhaps this has something to do with the fact that, as the Apostles preached throughout the Mediterranean world, the New Testament as we have it did not even exist.

How does one build on the foundation of the Apostles and the Prophets with Jesus as a chief cornerstone? Teachers and preachers would often comment that we do that today by reading, studying, and applying the words that they left for us in Scripture. I would not deny that, but I would not stop there either for the Apostles, the Prophets, even Jesus himself, were more than their ideas. I am more than my ideas, and so are you. I am more than my words, and so are you. These ancient men and women are no different. Step back, though, and ask, "What do we call the body of apostles, prophets, evangelists, and teachers, gathered together in line with Jesus of Nazareth?" Is this not the church? It is this church, then, that is the real foundation and storehouse of the truth itself. Again, this seems to be the understanding of St. Paul as he wrote to Timothy:

> *"I hope to come to you soon, but I am writing these instructions to you so that, if I am delayed, you may know how one ought to behave in the household of God, which is the church of the living God, the pillar and bulwark of the truth."*[21]

---

21 1 Tim 3:14–15.

3. How do you read these instructions?

Truly, it is the church which is the pillar and foundation of the truth, not Scripture alone. This does not undermine the importance of Scripture, though, far from it! To be sure, Scripture exists today as the church's primary witness to the truth. Yet, seeing as how Scripture developed as a witness to the truth, we will fail to interpret Scripture properly if we attempt to do so all by itself separate and detached from the ecclesial context in which it developed.

There are examples in Scripture of this principle at work. Consider the story of the Eunuch from Ethiopia who traveled to worship in Jerusalem in Acts 8. We are not told in Scripture if this was his first trip to Jerusalem or if this was something he regularly did. At any rate, on his return trip from Jerusalem, he had secured a copy of the text of Isaiah. This by itself is impressive for the Jewish Scriptures at this time would have had to be hand-copied and passed on at some considerable cost. Yet, here he was traveling back to the court of Queen Candice reading from the book of Isaiah – what we know as chapter 53. Philip, by the prompting of the Holy Spirit, goes up to him and asks, "Do you understand what you're reading?" The Eunuch replied, "How can I, unless someone guides me?"[22]

What he admitted, what we often fail to admit, is that meaning is not often self-evident, nor is it singular. Considering Isaiah 53 as a test case, there is the meaning that Isaiah had in mind when he wrote it, this we'll call the authorial intent. There is the mean-

---

22   Acts 8:31.

ing defined in the way his audience received it, we'll call this initial reception, and there is yet a third meaning appropriated by Christian sources. Christians, like Philip in this case, think Isaiah 53 is a text about the salvific work of the Passion of Jesus on Golgotha. Jews, however, surely would not make that same assumption even though they're reading the same text. Additionally, Isaiah's first readers probably didn't have many Jesus thoughts rolling around in their heads either. So what is the text really about? Well, we have to admit that it would depend not only on context but also on the list of assumptions one brings to the interpretive table. This is why the Eunuch needed Phillip. He needed one who was enlightened to share his illumination into the Christian reading of Israel's Scriptures. What we see, albeit in infancy, is the beginnings of a Christian tradition of reading Scripture.

It was this growing Tradition that brought Paul into the Faith. True, it was Jesus who corrected his path, but Jesus directed him to a real person in Damascus to learn what to do. Once there, a real person instructed him laying his hands on him as he was illumined to an even greater extent by the Holy Spirit. In these moments, Paul abandoned the traditions of his fathers (Galatians 1:14) and came to warn his students about the traditions of men (Col. 2:8). However, far from repudiating tradition, on the whole, he merely traded these traditions for what he considered to be a superior tradition based on a real experience of the divine. He would go on to encourage the brethren to *"stand firm and hold to the traditions* which you were

3. How do you read these instructions?

taught by us, either by word of mouth or by letter."[23] Furthermore, later in that same letter, he added, "Now we command you, brethren, in the name of our Lord Jesus Christ, that you keep away from any brother who is living in idleness and *not in accord with the tradition that you received from us.*"[24] Again, what we see here is the development of a Christian reading of Scripture that is passed down from the group of those initially enlightened (e.g., Apostles) to subsequent generations of people coming to faith in Jesus.

What I came to realize, and what I am suggesting here, is that the Bible cannot be interpreted correctly all by itself. Just as words need context, the Bible itself needs the Christian Tradition as a context to define the Scripture it produced. Within this Tradition, long before far-reaching schisms in the tradition itself, there is a rich history of interpretational tools such as creeds, particularly the Nicene Creed and the Apostles Creed, along with writings of early church fathers and apologists. It is far beyond the scope of this little book to make a case for the appropriate place of Creeds and the writings of Church Fathers in our understanding of Scripture, but, again, there are far more learned voices than mine who can help you connect these dots.[25] Yes, I still confess the words of 2 Timothy 3:16-17. I still believe that "All scripture is

---

23 2 Thess 2:15 (emphasis mine).
24 2 Thess 3:6 (emphasis mine).
25 Some of the most helpful voices on this are Robert Jenson, *Canon and* Creed: Resources for the Use of Scripture in the Church. (WJK Press, 2010), McDonald and Sanders, *The Canon Debate,* (Hendrickson, 2008), and Khaled Anatolios, *Retrieving Nicaea,* (Baker Academic, 2011)

inspired by God and profitable for teaching, for reproof, for correction, and for training in righteousness, that the man of God may be complete, equipped for every good work." [26] But, I also understand now that the Scripture to which Paul referred, could not have been the New Testament for it didn't yet exist neither can "profitable" mean "sufficient in and of itself." Just as our Lord said in John 5:31 ("If I bear witness to myself, my testimony is not true"), the Bible doesn't bear witness to itself as the final chief authority.

Finally, I realize how scandalous these words may sound. Still, the truth of that matter when it comes to biblical interpretation is simply this. When we start with the presumption that the Scriptures alone are God's communication from Heaven to humanity and that it is up to us to figure out His intentions therein and apply them to our everyday life, we are going to be faced with inconsistences and abuses no matter what interpretational strategy we use for we have begun the entire enterprise on a faulty premise. If we begin with thinking the Bible is God's speech to us, then we have no other option but to argue with one another about what it all means and fight amongst ourselves concerning our respective conclusions. Such a model would look an awful lot like the current religious landscape of our post-Reformation World as Christians divide themselves around their particular interpretations of "thus saith the Lord." The way through the difficulties of CENI, the issues of silence,

---

26   2 Tim 3:16–17.

3. How do you read these instructions?

or any other interpretational idiosyncrasies so frequent in the conservative RM churches is not found in stubborn debate but rather in the humble acknowledgment that there is much more to the story than what was originally suspected. The path through is found in the confession that knowing the truth is not the same as knowing the whole truth. We need the continuum of church history in its fullness to grasp the bearing and content of Scripture itself, for, without it, we are left in an interpretational ocean on a sea of words with our thinking as our best guide.

4.
Will the Real Church Members Please Stand Up?

I like to know what I'm working with when I have a task to do. Our house has numerous trees around it, and the leaves are a perpetual problem. I can rake, I can use a leaf blower, and it doesn't matter most days. Between the wind and all the oaks, the leaves spend more time on my grass than they should. However, when it's time to remove them, I set a goal. I'm going from the driveway to the porch swing and out to the road. That's day one. As long as I know my boundaries, I can deal with it. I approach most problems like that. Sometimes one of my kids will come to me with a problem, and I most often say, "Let's make a list of what might reasonably happen." After we construct that list, I'll encourage them to identify the worst-case scenario and then find a way to make peace with that. I do this because, if you can make peace with the worst case, then anything else is gravy. In my experience, knowing your boundaries usually works wonders.

Sadly, however, finding my way in the churches of Christ, I was often alarmed by the blurry nature of church boundaries – the boundaries that may have mattered the most. I'll give you a few examples. Our church used to make these directories that had everyone's birthday or anniversary along with their address and other pertinent information. I'm not knocking the idea; in fact, most churches probably do that. But what made our church directory interesting, to me anyway, was how the number of people on the directory was so much higher than the number of people in the pews any given Sunday. I'm sure most people would just chalk this up to normalcy; isn't that how all churches are? But for me, ever the inquisitor that I was, I studied that directory and asked, "Why aren't they here?" My mother or father would reply, "Well, they're not members here. They are just related to people who are, and since they are so close to us, we include them because people might want to send them a card." That's nice enough, I thought. But it also prompted me to examine just what it meant to be a "member."

Membership had to mean more than simply having your name on a directory. I mean, there were people on that list who I had never seen. I did my usual routine of asking and reading, and the answer I was offered went something like this. A person is a "member of the church" when he or she is baptized (full immersion, of course) for the remission of their

4. Will the Real Church Members Please Stand Up?

sins. (I should add here that the phrase "member of the church" or "member of the Lord's church" is in many RM circles used to identify those who are members of the church of Christ as opposed to regular church-going people.) Their description of membership seemed simple enough at first, but at second glance, there is a problem with that. Some of those people that were on our directory but were not members had been baptized in other contexts. The question remained. "Well," said my teachers, "it's not that simple, you see. Baptism is a tricky thing, so we have to make sure it's all on the up and up, so we like to see it performed by one of our faithful ministers. We just can't take their word for it; it's too important." I can respect that because I believe baptism is important; that all made sense. Still, there seemed to be many people out there who were doing just that same thing and, for some reason, were not counted in our tally. For the time being, I was content to dwell there at peace.

The problem became more complicated, as I recall, in two distinct moments. First, there was a family that had moved to our church from a neighboring church across town and attended with some regularity for several months. One Sunday, the patriarch of the family announced that they wished to become members there. Some in the congregation welcomed them with open arms and said, "Welcome!" My father, on the other hand, said, in so many words, "Not so fast!" All the tense moments aside, I was secretly joyed because I thought I was going to finally understand what it meant to be a member of the church.

Either these people are in, or they are out, right? Funny thing, I never really learned what happened. They had some closed doors meetings, and I was never privy to what they discussed. I do remember, however, that not much changed after that. They still came. They even took part in the services sometimes. I guess they were members?

As I grew, especially after my preaching stint started, I became more aware of what went on in those closed-door meetings. It was what amounted to several men sitting around a table in some form of pseudo-democracy. In my experience, there were never many men who wanted to be there but were all there through some sense of duty to the goings-on of the church. I should pause here and inform some of you who may not know about these "business meetings" as they were called. In the churches of Christ that I ran with, women were not allowed in the decision-making progress. Of course, there was Scripture for that.[27] Mind you; this was not the official teaching of the church. The official teaching (read here the teaching found in the books and journals) was that each church was to be governed autonomously by a group of elders and deacons as *clearly* outlined in Scripture.[28] However, smaller churches, like nearly all the ones with which I was affiliated, never had the human resources available to "qualify" anyone. Taking instruction from the qualifications for bishops and

---

27 It's actually debatable. It comes down to how you read that silence issue which is a whole different book.
28 Most commonly used Scriptures are 1 Tim. 3:1-13, Tit. 1:5-9, and 1 Pet. 5:1-5.

4. Will the Real Church Members Please Stand Up?

deacons in Scripture, 1 Timothy 3, for example, most often left churches with "unqualified" people to serve in these important leadership roles. And so, in their absence, there were business meetings ran by the "men" of the congregation. Men, in this case, being those males who were baptized and were considered "church members." (Even though that term is a little fuzzy at this point.)

In this pseudo-democracy, someone would bring up an issue, and it would be discussed. Most of the time, the items were rather mundane, having to do with cleaning or upkeep on the grounds. Occasionally, they tracked towards matters of Christian living and practice, and now and then, a theological argument may be made in support or against an issue. In one such meeting, I recall bringing up the idea of this directory as a means of figuring out who was a member there. Strange as it may seem, no one knew where to draw the line. I was concerned at the time that there were members who weren't coming and who needed to be ministered to, and it fell to us, as masters of the business meeting, to make contact with these missing people. The trouble was, as I learned, we didn't always know whom to minister to. This raised yet another question.

There was one interaction of importance in these meetings that I remember clearly. "Suppose," I interjected, "I went out into the streets and found eight men who I brought to church, taught them the gospel, and baptized them." The seven men that were there for that meeting exclaimed, "That'd be great!" "Well, not so fast," I replied. "If I baptized eight men tomorrow, would they not have as much right to come to this business meeting as us? And if that's the case, we'd be in the minority! Suppose those eight men decided to introduce instrumental music and communion on Tuesday, they'd win because there are eight of them and seven of us! What will we do about that?" I know some congregations who write church defining issues like these into the covenants for the deed to the church property, so major theological issues quickly become more complex legal issues. While this is fancy legal footwork to make sure things stay the same at a particular location, it doesn't go that far in helping anything else.

I remember the room being silent. I thought for a moment, at least, that I had finally conveyed the seriousness of the issue at hand, which was, as a congregation, we had no clue where our boundaries were. We didn't have a good idea who was in and who wasn't, and we surely had no real vision for tomorrow. To be sure, this is not an isolated problem. I preached at dozens of smaller congregations across the state of West Virginia who all fit this same pattern. These congregations, due to limits of their biblical interpretation, were frozen in a curious state unable to adapt or defend themselves in a particular context. Even to this day, this saddens me, for there are good people in these congregations who are genuine examples of Christian love frozen by poor interpretations of Scripture. These are fine examples of humanity, generosity, kindness, love, and peace, and these people, as good as they are, are sheep without a shepherd. Too many times, I witnessed a shepherd

4. Will the Real Church Members Please Stand Up?

arise who had promise and hope only to devour a few more and leave congregations worse off than before. At times, I think I may have been one too. However, I'm afraid that, unless the current changes directions, that will continue to happen. There is something about that context that just breeds that sort of thing.

As I mentioned above, I like to have defined boundaries when dealing with just about anything. When it came to church, however, I was never able to get that. I never knew who was really in or out or where you even drew the line. When given the standard answer, no one ever agreed on the objections. There seemed to be no consistent way to apply the "simple truth" they so boldly gleaned from their hermeneutic. Sadly, too often, the line was drawn far too conservatively, in my opinion, which left a trail of hurt feelings, confusion, and pain in the wake. I remember studying with a friend in college who was moving to live in California, and I was attempting to help him find a church there. This proved quite difficult because I was never able to answer the membership question. What if the church he meets up with counts things differently than I do? It's not just as simple as finding a new church with the same name on the door. Although the name might be the same, what's inside can vary wildly, not just in West Virginia but across the globe! I never knew what to tell him.

Even more recently, just before our exit from the churches of Christ, my wife, who was baptized just like me except for the location, was given some sort of provisional membership, which I didn't even know existed. This congregation had elders and deacons, and they decided to let us both be members there but that she was unable to do anything unless she consented to be re-baptized in a church of Christ building. Some preachers told me that you must be baptized for the remission of sins to be a member of the church. I asked what about all those who did that, but they weren't in a church of Christ building? Some said it didn't matter, some said it did, and some had no clue how to answer that. What I was a part of was a group of people that insisted on radical autonomy. Given that, why should we be surprised that there was never any consistent answers to important questions? They had built a structure that reinforced individual opinion versus brotherhood wide consensus.

This leads me to another eye-opening question. Even if you could solve the membership puzzle, what would that even mean? Growing up, being a member meant that you could take weekly communion. However, nearly everyone did anyway, member or not. It also meant that, if you were male, you could go to the business meeting, which is a rabbit trail, we will not tread anymore. If you were male, it also meant that you could lead prayers, preach, serve at the communion table, and lead singing. Women, although they did all the same things required of all people to become members, were not allowed to be seen as leaders in any way. Taking this to the issue at hand, then, what separated women members from nonmembers of any gender? It seems that in many cases, female members and nonmembers, in general, enjoyed the

4. Will the Real Church Members Please Stand Up?

same privileges. I have never received a valid answer to these questions because they always seem to get mired in deeper questions about how we read the Bible in the first place.

I struggled with questions about not only who was in the church and who wasn't but also how that status was affected and with what it was affected. I know that some people may think this question is rooted in judgmentalism. I mean, who am I to decide who's in or out? However, it's important to note that I'm not submitting these questions from the position of a prospective gatekeeper. I have always just wanted to understand where the line was that someone had to cross to go from not being a "member of the Lord's church" to being one. Even more, once one was a "member of the Lord's church," what did that even mean? Were there membership advantages? Did it just entitle you to be able to do church things in public? In other words, where are the boundary lines of "the church?" If there was no perceptible change or meaning, did church membership even mean anything substantive at all?

Before going further, I want to attempt to get on the same page concerning what we mean when we say "church." In my experience, much confusion can arise when we attempt to clarify what we mean we say "church." This is due, in part, to the reality of that word, for we use it in different ways to mean various things. I'm not trying to convince you here that you should change your definition of the church; I am merely clarifying what I mean when I use the phrase. Hopefully, this will make the cloudy waters somewhere clearer. I hope it goes without saying that, at the very least, I am referring to people in this context, not a building, when I use the word church.

When describing the word "church," we often add the modifier "universal." Concerning the phrase "universal church," some imagine an assembly of people with unseen boundaries made up of only true believers across time and space whose names are recorded in heaven in the Book of Life added only by the Lord himself.[29] This, according to some estimation, is *the* one true church; to many, this is "the Lord's Church." Still, others thinking of the universal church think of the church on Earth but broadly speaking, using the term to talk about the church as a whole of which the local church is only a small subset. In the second sense, people are often concerned about identifying themselves with the particular subset, which they feel most accurately represents the one *true* church in heaven as it pertains to doctrine and practice. As we continue, just for the sake of clarity, I'll use "universal church" in the first sense.

Church leaders, at least in my experience, taught that the universal church, in the first sense, was the real membership that counted as well as the true definition of church. Perhaps that's why they never really worried so much about keeping another essentially inferior list in writing or even worrying too much about the boundaries at all. I mean, after all, the real list is God's business, right? The only real boundary issues, at least in their minds, were the details of

---

29   Acts 2:42

4. Will the Real Church Members Please Stand Up?

one's baptism primarily and one's doctrinal stances on some key issues. These doctrinal stances were never consistent, though, and too broad to address here. As many of you may know, this issue is exacerbated in congregations with no official leadership. In that case, who's to say who's in or who's out or what that even means?

Due to the uncertainty in definitions, people are left with the difficult task of trying to differentiate between the local church and the universal church and what it means to be a member of either. For example, when one became a member of local Church X in city Y, are they merely joining themselves to Church X, or was it the church in a universal sense? And if the matter wasn't complicated enough, many churches of Christ did not make a distinction at all between themselves the one Church in the Bible ("universal church") and, therefore, to be a member of one was to be a member of everything. To be sure, charges of elitism and "you think you're the only ones going to heaven" were leveled against the churches of Christ for this very reason. When people fail to provide reasonable answers concerning what church membership means, this can create significant problems.

Is it not important, though, as local congregations, to strive to emulate the church we read of in the Bible? Indeed, this is the mission of the RM churches. They seek, for a good reason, to be the church that we read about in the New Testament. But is that possible? Have they done it? Has anyone? Like most things, it depends on definitions, which leads back to a central issue in this book. If we define continuity with first-century Christianity solely as doctrinal agreement, which is the primary emphasis in churches of Christ, then being the first-century church is possible insofar as we can reconstruct first-century teaching. However, as I have already suggested elsewhere, continuity with the first-century church covers, I think, a broader spectrum than doctrinal agreement alone. Let me explain.

Consider the question, "Where is the Lord's church?" If we define "Lord's church" as the group of the Lord's disciples, then, in the gospel accounts, the church is where the Lord is. That is to say that wherever Jesus is, the church is there because they were the group of people who reacted positively to his command, "follow me." I know some may object to this because of the grammar of Matthew 16:18, where Jesus said, "I will build my church." I understand that this building project announcement uses a future tense verb indicating that the establishment of the church had not yet happened. Again, we have a definition issue here.

The word "church," or ἐκκλησία (ecclesia), is not something that Jesus invented in the first century. In the Greek version of the Old Testament, the Septuagint (c. 3rd Century BCE), the word is often used of the assembly of Israel in the Old Testament. Take Deuteronomy 31:30, 1 Sam. 17:47, or Psalm 22:22 for example, where ἐκκλησία (ecclesia) lays behind words like assembly or congregation.[30] So, in the time

---

[30] See also the instance ἐκκλησία of Acts 7:38 in which Stephen refers to the "congregation of Israel."

4. Will the Real Church Members Please Stand Up?

of Jesus, it would not be strange at all for the Jews to be collectively called the ἐκκλησία of which both Jesus himself and his disciples were part of. This ἐκκλησία had definite boundaries marked out primarily by circumcision, monotheistic devotion to the God of Israel, and worship of that God as prescribed by the Law of Moses at the Temple in Jerusalem. But even that may be saying too much.

Judaism was somewhat splintered in Jesus' time. There were different strands of Judaism that often stood at odds with one another. The Pharisees and Sadducees didn't see eye to eye on all matters, particularly the nature of the Law itself, angels, and the resurrection. Zealots opposed the Roman occupation of Judea, and The Herodian party supported Rome in alliance with the Pharisees (Mark 3:16, 12:13). There was also the Essenes who turned their backs on all the perceived corruption and error and started their community in the desert. Due to the splintering, as well as the diaspora across the Mediterranean world, perhaps Temple worship was not even a defining trait of Judaism in the ancient world as it has not been since 70 AD when Rome destroyed the Temple.

It is important to think about the nature of the Jewish world to which Jesus and his disciples ministered as they preached about the coming of the Kingdom of God. As Jesus and his disciples accused hypocritical teachers, exposed vain worship and traditions which had supplanted the truth, people began to raise the same sort of question we are raising here. That is, who is really in this congregation of Lord's faithful? The Jewish answer, so it seems, had to do both with one's birth and with one's allegiances to the teachers in one's synagogue. But then here is Jesus and his disciples preaching a message that true belonging in the family of God was not a function of fleshly birth, but a spiritual birth. (cf. John 3) Additionally, they were teaching that you could boil the whole law down to two laws; Love God and Love your neighbor. (cf. Matt. 22:34-40) As people began to listen to what Jesus said and take notice of what He was doing, some people expressed a desire to follow Him. To them, Jesus called for a total renouncing of the self and to "take up their cross and follow." (Luke 14:25-33) So, it seems, membership in this small community gathered around Jesus had more to do with self-sacrificing love for God and neighbor than birthright or political alignment. Even in this time, if we asked, "where is the church," you would get different answers depending on whom you talked to. Jews, depending on their affiliations, would say it is the nation of Israel. Jesus, however, would open his arms and say, "Behold my brothers and my sisters." (Matt. 12:46-50)

Where is the *true* church? Where is the *true* Israel? (Rom. 2:28-29) These questions, in the time of Jesus, were the same question. I believe the message of the gospels to be saying that the true church is where Jesus is for Jesus is the *true* Israel. This point is especially made clear in Matthew's Gospel. Israel passed through the Red Sea into the Wilderness, faced the conquest, and recoiled in fear, but Jesus passed through the Jordan in his baptism and went into the wilderness facing the Devil and defeated the enemy.

4. Will the Real Church Members Please Stand Up?

Next, Jesus goes up on the Mountain to speak about Torah just as Moses had gone up on the mountain to deliver the Law. On the one hand, Israel went into the Promised Land and consistently failed to live up to the standard of Torah being all that God wanted them to be. But Jesus, on the other hand, lives the Law perfectly, being all that humanity is supposed to be. In remembrance of the Exodus, the Jews sacrificed a Passover lamb, but Jesus, our Passover lamb, sacrificed Himself once and for all in *His* exodus.[31] When the Jews in the time of Moses failed to cross the river and conquer their enemy, Jesus, through death, crossed over and defeated the true enemy of all humanity – death itself. Reading the life of Jesus is reading the life of Israel as it should have been if they were loyal to God's word. This is possible because Jesus *is* the Word of God enfleshed. (cf. John 1)

In what way, if any, did Jesus' ascension change this? In some sense, Christians have always confessed that while Jesus is not here in the flesh, He is still here amongst his disciples. Jesus, speaking to his followers in Matthew 28, said, "I will be with you always, even unto the end of the age." Even though the disciples did not seem to fully grasp the complexity of Jesus' leaving, they were introduced to the idea probably on the day, at least, before the crucifixion. In Jesus' long discourse covering John 14-18, Jesus speaks about his departure and the coming of "another comforter." (cf. John 14:16-17) This comforter is none other than the Holy Spirit, who is described using the word, in Eng-

---

[31] See "departure" of Jesus in Luke 9:30-31. The Greek behind departure is ἔξοδον (exodus).

lish, another. Reading John 14 leaves one with at least three important impressions. First, Jesus is leaving. (cf. John 14:1-14) Second, his leaving should not be understood as an absence for he said,

> *"I will pray the Father, and he will give you another Counselor, to be with you for ever, even the Spirit of truth, whom the world cannot receive, because it neither sees him nor knows him; you know him, for he dwells with you, and will be in you."*[32]

And third, the coming of the Holy Spirit and his continued dwelling with the community gathered around Jesus *was to be understood* as Jesus' continued presence in the community for the Holy Spirit of God is the same Spirit in Jesus. (John 3:34-36) Jesus continued,

> *"I will not leave you desolate; I will come to you. Yet a little while, and the world will see me no more, but you will see me; because I live, you will live also. In that day you will know that I am in my Father, and you in me, and I in you. He who has my commandments and keeps them, he it is who loves me; and he who loves me will be loved by my Father, and I will love him and manifest myself to him."*[33]

---

32 John 14:15–17.
33 John 14:18–21.

4. Will the Real Church Members Please Stand Up?

Truly, Jesus did come to dwell among his people, albeit not in the same way as He had in the past. In those final days, Jesus taught that his presence among his people, his mission among the people, and his love for humanity would be continued by his disciples as they are filled with the Holy Spirit. So, back to our question, once Jesus ascended, where do we find the church? If the church was the community gathered around Christ, and the Holy Spirit is the continuity of His presence, then the church after the ascension is the community gathered in the name of Christ by the power of the Holy Spirit.

I think it's critical to pause here and make an observation. When Jesus was preparing to leave in the flesh, he emphasized two separate but vital truths. On the one hand, He taught them about the importance of continuity in their actions. That is, once He had ascended, He expected His disciples to continue to live the same lifestyle as taught before His ascension.

> *"If a man loves me, he will keep my word, and my Father will love him, and we will come to him and make our home with him."*[34]

On the other hand, however, He also expected them, based on their cooperation with the Holy Spirit, to grow in their understanding and grasp things that Jesus had not yet taught them.

---

34 John 14:23.

> "I have yet many things to say to you, but you cannot bear them now. When the Spirit of truth comes, he will guide you into all the truth; for he will not speak on his own authority, but whatever he hears he will speak, and he will declare to you the things that are to come. He will glorify me, for he will take what is mine and declare it to you. All that the Father has is mine; therefore I said that he will take what is mine and declare it to you."[35]

The disciples, it seems, did not understand everything that Jesus had taught. But, through the Spirit, Jesus would continue to teach his disciples even in his physical absence. In other words, the post-resurrection church would have continuity with the presence of Christ in the Spirit as well as continuity with His teaching and mission. Instead of stopping with that, however, the post-resurrection community would be a community of growth and development under the direction of the Holy Spirit as they came to a full understanding of the incarnate word of God.

The two separate but essential markers of continuity and growth are demonstrated throughout the book of Acts. Primarily, the community demonstrated its continuity in a public way on Pentecost in Acts 2. Through Peter's preaching, the community, at first numbering 120, began to grow. Notice, though, that people were being added to the community (i.e., church, the True Israel) as they both accepted the

---

35 John 16:12–15.

4. Will the Real Church Members Please Stand Up?

apostolic preaching and received the Holy Spirit in baptism.

> *"Now when they heard this they were cut to the heart, and said to Peter and the rest of the apostles, "Brethren, what shall we do?" And Peter said to them, "Repent, and be baptized every one of you in the name of Jesus Christ for the forgiveness of your sins; and you shall receive the gift of the Holy Spirit. For the promise is to you and to your children and to all that are far off, every one whom the Lord our God calls to him." And he testified with many other words and exhorted them, saying, "Save yourselves from this crooked generation." So, those who received his word were baptized, and there were added that day about three thousand souls."*[36]

And so, not only is continuity with Christ preserved in the Holy Spirit, continuity with his teaching is preserved in the Apostolic proclamation of salvation in Jesus' name. And in this teaching, the church continued:

> *"And they devoted themselves to the apostles' teaching and fellowship, to the breaking of bread and the prayers. And fear came upon every soul; and many wonders and signs were done through the apostles. And*

---

36 Acts 2:37–41.

> *all who believed were together and had all things in common; and they sold their possessions and goods and distributed them to all, as any had need. And day by day, attending the temple together and breaking bread in their homes, they partook of food with glad and generous hearts, praising God and having favor with all the people. And the Lord added to their number day by day those who were being saved."*[37]

Consequently, as you move through the book of Acts, and try to find "the church," you always find it gathered around leadership, namely Apostles, rejoicing in the presence of Christ in the Spirit, and sharing that joy with the rest of creation. Indeed, the church in Acts, as it was gathered around the Apostles and growing in both knowledge and understanding, was the "true Israel" because of its being in Christ, who was the "true Israel."

In the churches of Christ with whom I was associated, locating this primitive church was the matter of first importance. However, the primary search was always conducted on the grounds of continuity in doctrine. They were always concerned with teaching the same things as the apostles taught. This process only ever went as far as the New Testament, though. After the Apostles, all had died, so the thinking went, the church went into apostasy and dwelt in the dark until the times of the RM. The church of the Bible, so

---

37 Acts 2:42–47.

4. Will the Real Church Members Please Stand Up?

they thought, was the perfect pattern, and, as such, we deviate from that pattern to our peril.

However, I believe that locating the *true* church in today's world using this blueprint approach is simply not possible, for it fails to appropriately value continuity with *all* the aspects of the original apostolic community, namely growth, focusing only on the doctrinal positions. To be truly continuous with the original apostolic community is to value not only continuity in the Spirit, but also growth in the Spirit for Jesus taught his disciples to expect both. First, concerning continuity in the Holy Spirit, consider the passages of Scripture that connect the spreading of the Church with the spreading of the Holy Spirit; Acts 8:14-17, Acts 10:44-48, and Acts 19:1-7. Interestingly, hearing the word and being baptized was not enough in these cases to produce acceptance into the community for representatives of the church needed to acknowledge their acceptance through the laying on of hands by which they shared in the Spirit. I am not suggesting that hearing the word of God and being baptized is not required, but I am suggesting that people who responded to the message sought acceptance and recognition by the church that they believed in Christ and accepted the Truth as the Apostles witnessed.

Secondly, concerning growth in the Spirit, it is not reasonable to look back into Acts and say what you're seeing is *the* pattern for what you're looking at is a snapshot in time, a static image of the Spirit-filled community. The church in Acts was a growing community, not just in numbers, but in an understanding of what it meant to bear the image of God in his good creation. A common objection that you hear sometimes is that the Apostles were set in the church fully grown and had a perfect understanding of things. Of course, you would have to believe that if you subscribed to the idea that the church in Acts is *the* perfect pattern. Oddly, I never heard anyone provide any biblical grounds for believing this idea. (Perhaps it's a "necessary" inference?) Yet, the church led by the Apostles experienced growing pains that would lead one to think that perhaps the Apostles were not set in the church "full-grown" or with "complete maturity."

Consider Peter, in Acts 10, as he was wrestling with the visions of the animals on the great sheet as a precursor to the ultimate issue of whether or not the church could include gentiles. Is Peter here, "full-grown?"

> "Now while Peter was inwardly perplexed as to what the vision which he had seen might mean, behold, the men that were sent by Cornelius, having made inquiry for Simon's house, stood before the gate and called out to ask whether Simon who was called Peter was lodging there. And while Peter was pondering the vision, the Spirit said to him, "Behold, three men are looking for you. Rise and go down, and accompany them without hesitation; for I have sent them."[38]

---

38   Acts 10:17–20.

4. Will the Real Church Members Please Stand Up?

Or does Peter exhibit "complete maturity" when he was caught in difficult issues concerning relationships between Jews and Gentiles?

> *"But when Cephas came to Antioch I opposed him to his face, because he stood condemned. For before certain men came from James, he ate with the Gentiles; but when they came he drew back and separated himself, fearing the circumcision party. And with him the rest of the Jews acted insincerely, so that even Barnabas was carried away by their insincerity. But when I saw that they were not straightforward about the truth of the gospel, I said to Cephas before them all, "If you, though a Jew, live like a Gentile and not like a Jew, how can you compel the Gentiles to live like Jews?"*[39]

To be sure, the church of the first century faced a difficult issue as they brought gentiles into the community, which was formerly exclusively Jew. So difficult was this issue that they had to get together and sort it out. Acts 15:1-30 records both the council proceedings and the subsequent letter written by the council that was to be delivered to the troubled brethren. It is interesting to note that the Apostles and Elders discussed with one another, reflected on Scripture (Old Testament, of course), and reasoned a course of action together. This does not appear to be the speech of

---

39   Gal. 2:11–14.

"full-grown" men speaking as the "pattern holders" for they wrote in the letter,

> "For it has seemed good to the Holy Spirit and to us to lay upon you no greater burden than these necessary things: that you abstain from what has been sacrificed to idols and from blood and from what is strangled and from unchastity. If you keep yourselves from these, you will do well. Farewell."[40]

Three times in Acts 15, we find the phrase "it seemed good to us." (Acts 15:22, 25, 28) "Seemed," from the Greek δοκεω, means "to appear to one's understanding, seem, or be recognized as."[41] That is to say, the pronouncements of that council were something the Apostles reasoned out together and, based on that discussion, decided on a new course of action. This does not mean that they did not speak with authority, however. It was the Apostles and Elders that gathered to make these decisions and not anyone else, but, and this is important, the Apostles did not speak for themselves – "it seemed good to us and the Holy Spirit." They were trusted as authoritative figures because of their relationship to Jesus in the Spirit, evidenced by word and deed.

The narrative often submitted by the churches of Christ is that the church went apostate after the apostles died until the time of the RM. This fails, I think,

---

40   Acts 15:28–29.
41   *BDAG*, (Chicago: University of Chicago Press, 2000), 255.

4. Will the Real Church Members Please Stand Up?

to realize the fact that the church in Acts was a church in infancy beginning to grapple with the truth of the Resurrected Lord and what it meant to be the true people of God. Although I think it's untenable, you could suppose, as many do, that the Apostles knew everything perfectly and had no room to grow, and when they died, imperfect people just came along and messed it all up. If you think that may be the case, then you have to wonder what makes us qualified to un-mess it all up? How would going back to the beginning fix anything? You might say that going back to the beginning means doing apostolic things in apostolic ways, but remember, it was the Holy Spirit that both gathered and led them, and we, in Christ, have that same Spirit.

Additionally, if one assumed that the Apostles were set in the church fully grown and completely mature and were keepers of the official God-approved pattern for worship and ethics, then you would also have to alter your understanding of growth. At the outset of this book, we admitted that growth into the truth of God was an infinite process because God Himself is infinite. If one can fully know all the truth, then how can God, who is the truth, be infinite? How, then, can we imagine a world where the Apostles were fully grown when, in any other estimation, we would deny the possibility of *anyone* being fully grown? I suppose one could confess that God did a miraculous thing with the Apostles and never again with anyone else, but you'd have to confess that with no evidence merely as a way to prop up a preconceived notion.

Let me suggest, finally, another more plausible narrative. The church in Acts was gathered, empowered, and led by the Holy Spirit and the Apostles were the representative and icons of that power. As the church grew in number and spirit, they faced new challenges, and together, under the apostolic leadership, they met those new challenges and found new ways forward. When false teachers arose, they turned people's attention back to the foundational truths that they understood in light of their relationship with Jesus in the Spirit. As the church continued to grow, even more, the apostles ordained other leaders (e.g., Presbyters, Bishops, Elders, Deacons) to protect the continuity in both spirit and doctrine while ensuring continued growth in number and spirit. It is easier, I think, to believe that this process never ended and never went dark. Surely, the church faced difficulties and met new challenges. In those times, they continued to meet in council after the manner of Acts 15 and sort these new issues out. Sometimes, cooler heads did not prevail, and schisms occurred, but through the Holy Spirit, Jesus never left his church. Restoration, then, is not the answer. Rather, what is needed is repentance, just as has always been the case.

Perhaps we should use the phrase "one true church" as a synonym for the family built on the Abrahamic promise to become a great nation blessing all the earth. This one family tree is the same vine taken out of Egypt and planted in Canaan. (Psalm 80) This is the same vine that failed to be the tree of life for the nations. (Isaiah 5) This is the same vine that

4. Will the Real Church Members Please Stand Up?

Jesus confessed to being truly himself. (John 15:1-11) This is the vine into which we are grafted by God's grace. (Rom. 11:16-24) Where is the church? The church, the true church, is where it has always been, gathered around the Lord, steadfast in the word of the Lord, living on His flesh and blood (John 6), and ever-growing as a fruit-bearing branch of the Vine Himself.

To close this chapter, I want to suggest one more time that a desire to restore the first-century church according to some ill-defined pattern is not only difficult but is destined to fail, for it fails to recognize the fundamental nature of the church. Far from a mere philosophy rooted in doctrines and dogmas, the church is the body of Christ, living, growing, and moving through time. It is not something we can restore; it is something we discover. Philosophies are lost and restored, true life is not. There is no repentance in a philosophy; either you're in or you're not. The Body of Christ, true life itself, instead, is not a set of dogmas to which we assent; it is a vine into which we are grafted. We do not support the root; the root supports us. (Rom. 11:18) Indeed He who is head over all things to the Church and who fills all in all has never left his people even when we made a mess of things. (Eph. 1:22-23) What is someone saying about Christ, then, when they say that the church fell apostate for 1700 years until faithful men restored the pattern on the 19th Century American frontier?

5.
Sir, Have You Heard the Gospel?

As I floated on down the stream with my church family, we often communicated with each other using standard catchphrases as most traditions do. One of the most popular phrases one might hear from members of the church involved "obeying the gospel."

"Let's rejoice, Mr. Smith has obeyed the gospel! He's now a child of God!"

"If you haven't obeyed the gospel, you need to!"

"I'm ready to obey the gospel!"

I know there was probably some preacher, or school of preachers, who popularized that phrase; it was too prevalent to be a natural development. In all probability, those early evangelists more than likely borrowed the phrase from one of three places in Scripture.[42] But what does it mean to obey the gospel?

---

42   Romans 10:16, 2 Thess. 1:8, or 1 Pet. 4:17

Naturally, I've wrestled with this question, and at times I rested, thinking I had bested that questions and laid it to rest. There was a time in my life when I, along with most other preachers in the churches of Christ, would have given the same answer. To obey the gospel, I reasoned, meant to be baptized. Humor me for a moment and let me explain my reasoning.

The Gospel, as Paul reviews it in 1 Corinthians 15, is the story of Jesus dying for our sins, being buried, resurrected, and then being seen by many in the ensuing days. It seems by this, and also by the fact that the gospel was something that Paul preached from town to town, that the gospel was essentially a story or a message about the salvific work. How one could obey this message needed some connective work. And so, the reasoning goes, you obey the message by reenacting the same story in your life. On one level, I can get behind that idea so long as the idea is enriched with greater detail about the all-encompassing work of God in Christ on the cross. However, in those days, it was never that broad. Reenacting that salvific event was essentially flattened to a single moment in time where a believer repented of their sins (death), and that dead former self was fully immersed in water (buried) and brought out of the water to a new life (resurrection). This line of thinking made the baptism event the event *par excellence* in the Christian's life. Without it, they were nothing; they were excluded from Christ, having never shared in his saving work. Without it, there were in danger of Hell's fire, having never had their sins washed away. This is what made

5. Sir, Have You Heard the Gospel?

the gospel so good – it was the message of a clean slate and eternal redemption.

I'm not trying to downplay the importance of baptism, the forgiveness of sins, eternal redemption, or the salvific work of Christ on the cross. Those things are of prime importance in the drama of salvation. Neither am I debating the place of baptism in the Christian's life. I preached that message for many years and still believe in "one baptism for the remission of sins."[43] However, after so many sermons and years of reflection, I did begin to think that the message of "obedience to the gospel" was somewhat one-dimensional. The message that I both preached and heard sounded to me like a simple binary question robed in religious regalia.

"Have you obeyed the gospel?"

"Why yes, yes, I have."

"Great! Next!"

I don't recall the exact time that I became aware of this reality. I suspect it crept up on me like a fox. Once it had its teeth in me, though, I couldn't help but struggle against it. Is that all there is to it? Dunk them and move on? Once you've been submerged, you're in? I never heard anyone explicitly say it just like that, though. To be sure, most preachers nearly always tacked on a verse from Revelation 2 that encouraged all the faithful to remain faithful until death. More on that later.

The one-dimensional gospel message, as I came to think of it, started to not feel so gospel-y. It failed, af-

---

[43] Statement about baptism in the Nicene-Constantinopolitan Creed.

ter years, to live up to the hype of real life-changing good news. That's what the gospel is supposed to mean, right? Good news? What's so good about it? This was the question I wrestled with for years more intently, though, after failed attempts at convincing people to obey the gospel. Why would anyone not obey it? It's good news! What's wrong with them? Why would anyone turn their nose up at the forgiveness of sins? Did they not know they were sinners? What even is a sinner?

Well, according to many of those in my circles, sin was more than just doing bad things like lying, cheating, stealing, and fornication. Although it was that for sure, sin, in their view, also had a mental, logical, element to it. That is, sin could be committed in thought and word, as well as in action. Many churches might agree with this if pressed, I don't know for sure, but in my context, one could sin by doing church differently than we did. So, we had figured we were worshipping and living according to the pattern of New Testament Christianity. We had obeyed the gospel of Christ! If you or your church was living/doing/worshipping differently, that is according to a different interpretation, then you/they were sinful and needed to repent and obey the gospel.

If you take this view of sin, however, it makes for a difficult sales pitch. Essentially, what I found myself doing in my preaching work was trying to convince people to read the bible in a certain way that cast my voice as the voice of truth and their preferred method of biblical interpretation as the fountainhead of corruption and sin. If I could convince them to read the

5. Sir, Have You Heard the Gospel?

Bible like me, then I could convince them of their sinfulness. If I could convince them of their sinfulness, then, as luck would have it, I had good news for them! All they needed to do was obey the gospel and do church as we did it, and all would be well between them and God! Easy, right?

Well, it's easy if you only see people who have a different interpretational approach than you as sinners. In this way, all the people in all the pews of all the other denominations had to be the sinful ones because they weren't reading and interpreting the Bible as we did, in the manner we were convinced any reasonable person must read it. So many times, it was those people who stood in the crosshairs of "gospel preaching" and took the brunt of pulpit attention. Gospel preachers were those who accused those in error, condemned the other crooked preachers, and exposed the false prophets. Funny, though, none of those people ever seemed to hear our sermons, not in my experience anyway. They never came repenting. They never shed tears of sorrow for their sins. It's like they weren't even reading the same Bible. Never mind the ones running the streets, of course. I never felt like we had anything to ever offer them.

To be honest, for most of my life, I never understood what was so good about the good news. I had never received it as good news. If I may be blunt, I remember taking the trip to the baptistery when I was a kid simply to avoid the fires of hell and get the right to take communion. It wasn't because I loved the Lord, I did not have a real sense of my sinfulness, and I did not comprehend the extent to which I and all humanity were complicit in the corruption of all creation. I just wanted to not burn for all eternity and get those crackers and juice on Sunday. Once that threat was averted, it was back to life as normal. This was my experience, and I know that it was not this way for everyone raised in the churches of Christ. May God be glorified for all those whose experience was different!

As I grew, I began to question that decision and wrestle with both my understanding of the gospel and the meaning of baptism and what "obedience to the gospel" even means. If I were a betting man, I'd wager that many people who were baptized in the churches of Christ at a young age wrestled with that same foe. As I walked that path, I thought about the death of Christ, the torture of the cross, the resurrection on the third day, and how all that related to me and my sins. What did his agonizing death have to do with my evil thoughts? With my lying? With my greed? With my pride? If God wanted to forgive me so badly, why didn't he just do it? Why should one suffer for me?

As I came to know through my reading and endless questions, I was asking questions about the atonement; how did Christ's death prove efficacious for sins? In the churches of Christ that I knew, the most frequently given answer went something like this. God is just, righteous, and holy. Given this, he just can't look over sin; it had to be punished. The punishment for breaking the law of God, being much greater than mortal law, is eternal death. Such is our fate, as sinners, that we have no offering to bring and

5. Sir, Have You Heard the Gospel?

no ability to help ourselves appease the all-encompassing wrath of God against us vile sinners. This is where, according to the story, Jesus came in. He came and lived a perfect life and offered Himself as a perfect sacrifice for all humankind's sins. Now, through obedience to his message, we can avail ourselves of Christ's sacrifice and vicarious death, knowing that His death was for us (read instead of us). Now God doesn't see our cold black hearts anymore; He only sees His Son, and thus, we find salvation. As I'm sure you know by now, I combed over that process with intense focus and worked it over in my mind from many different angles. Accordingly, as I'm sure you're expecting, I had questions.

First, I never really could come to peace with the idea that God was so appalled by our sin that, when we did inevitably sin, he recoiled in wrath and removed himself from our presence. "Gospel Preachers" would at this time roll out Isaiah 59:1-2 saying, "Behold, the Lord's hand is not shortened, that it cannot save, or his ear dull, that it cannot hear; but your iniquities have made a separation between you and your God, and your sins have hid his face from you so that he does not hear."[44] I understood what this passage is saying, I just never quite wrapped my head around why they used it at this point. For starters, it's an Old Testament verse, and this violated the laws of New Testament Christianity 101. If I had a nickel for every time I heard that we could not take our instruction for life and worship from the Old Tes-

---

44   Isaiah 59:1–2

tament, I'd not need to work! But yet, here we are. Sometimes they'd even roll out part of Habakkuk 1:13 and call to our Lord as, "Thou who art of purer eyes than to behold evil and canst not look on wrong..."[45] leaving us with the impression that God recoiled at the sight of sin and abandoned all who were enslaved therein. For some reason, however, they left out the part of that verse that clearly said that he *did* see humanity in their sins! They would note the cry of our Lord from the cross and cry themselves in the person of the sinner, "My God! My God, why have you forsaken me?" Yet, they didn't seem to want to read the rest of Psalm 22, the source of Jesus' cry, which runs against the idea that God would abandon us in the time of need.

The God of abandonment did not seem to be the God of Eden. Who, in dealing with Adam and Eve's sin, did not abandon them but rather clothed them with animal skins after their failed attempt with fig leaves. There were consequences, of course, but never abandonment.[46] The God of those sermons was not the God of Cain, who, although he murdered his brother, was protected by a mark from God and a promise of retribution to all those who would afflict him.[47] This was not the God who, in Jesus, ate with sinners, tax collectors, prostitutes, and hypocrites. This was not the God who, according to St. Paul, was

---

[45] This is from Habakkuk 1:13. Interestingly, read the whole verse as well as the context. Most preachers I heard only quoted the first part.
[46] Genesis 3
[47] Genesis 4

5. Sir, Have You Heard the Gospel?

made to be sin for us.[48] Neither was this the God of the incarnation who became flesh to save us. As a youth, I was taught about a God who seemed only to tolerate me while I was on my best behavior and who was otherwise repulsed by the sins He knew I would commit. Worse still, I was taught that this was love. Where is the good news in this?

Remaining still was the nagging suspicion that something was lacking; is this all salvation is? Dallas Willard, wrestling with this same problem, came to call it "the gospel of sin management." Is the gospel merely a new law to help me behave more appropriately? Is the gospel simply a safety net for when I mess up? Or is the gospel merely the good news of God's willingness to tolerate us? I had no definitive answers, but I felt for sure that the one possible answer I had wasn't right. If I'm perfectly transparent here, at this time, I had no idea what the gospel was, and yet I was preaching it week in and week out. Sometimes I wonder what I was saying in those sermons. My best guess is that it was merely regurgitated tidbits that I had devoured over the years repurposed in what I thought was new and clever ways. If this is true, then by my message, God should have been far from me. He certainly shouldn't have been looking at me or even concerned at all with my activity being the sinner that I surely was. He shouldn't have been watching out for me, yet ironically, He was present in direct contradiction to the message I was delivering. The more I messed up, the more I came to

---

48 2 Cor. 5:21

see God's hand working behind the scenes, and it didn't appear to depend on my proper behavior as a prerequisite at all. Surely there must be more to this story than the confusing parts I thought I knew. If you were asked to articulate the gospel, could you do so with clarity? Could you explain why it is good news to people who, at the same time, do not understand sin?

I want to suggest here that the issue of all issues is the gospel, and being able to articulate the gospel with precision and grace is of prime importance not only for church leaders but for people in the pew as well. I admit that I had difficulty with this, for I often wondered what was so good about the news I had been taught. What I have come to realize is that a faulty way of reading scripture and an emaciated understanding of what the church is had left me blind to the real kernel of gospel truth. I knew enough, I suppose, to know there had to be something else. For that reason, I want to suggest in this chapter, that a broader, more complete, understanding of the gospel should be *the* foundational truth of our shared Christian identity.

Since "good" is a comparative word, understanding the "good" is possible as we juxtapose the "good" news with the "bad" news. First, let's hear the bad news. The bad news is the present human condition. It is almost universally recognized that the world and its inhabitants are flawed and broken, and no matter how hard we try, we can't seem to fix ourselves. People try to fix themselves with various aids, some of which are healthy (hobbies, careers, etc.) and some

5. Sir, Have You Heard the Gospel?

not so healthy (Drugs, alcohol, etc.). It seems that no matter how hard we try to put our lives together, we will end up making a mess of things to some degree. The Christian interpretation of this problem says that we cannot put ourselves back together because we are missing an important piece; God. As Blaise Pascal, supposedly, famously quipped, "There is a God-shaped vacuum in the heart of every man which cannot be filled by any created thing, but only by God, the Creator, made known through Jesus." Nice thought, but Pascal never said that. What he actually wrote is far more astute.

I quote Pascal here at length because I believe that he succinctly summarizes the human condition. He begins section 425 of his book, *Pensées*, with the following observation:[49]

> *"All men seek happiness. This is without exception. Whatever different means they employ, they all tend to this end. The cause of some going to war, and of others avoiding it, is the same desire in both, attended with different views. The will never takes the least step but to this object. This is the motive of every action of every man, even of those who hang themselves. And yet after such a great number of years, no one without faith has reached the point to which all continually look. All complain, princes and subjects,*

---

[49] "Pascal's Pensees." The Project Gutenberg eBook of Pascal's *Pensées*, by Blaise Pascal. Accessed May 13, 2020. https://www.gutenberg.org/files/18269/18269-h/18269-h.htm.

> *noblemen and commoners, old and young, strong and weak, learned and ignorant, healthy and sick, of all countries, all times, all ages, and all conditions. A trial so long, so continuous, and so uniform, should certainly convince us of our inability to reach the good by our own efforts. But example teaches us little. No resemblance is ever so perfect that there is not some slight difference; and hence we expect that our hope will not be deceived on this occasion as before. And thus, while the present never satisfies us, experience dupes us, and from misfortune to misfortune leads us to death, their eternal crown."*

The quote famously attributed to Pascal is fairly close to what Pascal is saying, but Pascal's actual words add an essential element that the quote misses. There is in all of us an unspoken draw to attend to this void, this absence of happiness and fulfillment. Isn't it strange how, in our way, we know this void exists, and we react with a primal instinct to address this felt absence in our life? Absence, though, can only be absence if something actually present at one time is now present no longer. Subsequently, we live with a nagging emptiness that we long to fill because something has been removed. Pascal continues:

> *"What is it then that this desire and this inability proclaim to us, but that there was once in man a true happiness of which there now remain to him only the mark and empty trace, which he in vain tries to fill from all*

5. Sir, Have You Heard the Gospel?

> *his surroundings, seeking from things absent the help he does not obtain in things present? But these are all inadequate because the infinite abyss can only be filled by an infinite and immutable object, that is to say, only by God Himself."*

Pascal makes sense because, like an artist, he accurately observes the condition of humanity and sees us all as we are. It makes sense; you can only fill an infinite void with an infinite object, but infinite voids can only be left where once the infinite object was. So, it seems, we mortals and eternity itself have a complicated history. And it is here that the gospel begins.

No doubt, we are familiar with the Genesis story detailing the creation of man and his "fall." Some people read this story as actual history while others read it allegorically; either way will work here because either way, it's the story of people made in the Image of God in a fellowship with God, unlike that which we can experience in this age. This communion continued for an uncertain amount of time until a force came along with a strange doctrine. This new doctrine was founded on the suggestion that maybe, just maybe, Adam and Eve had misinterpreted what God meant when he said, "you shall surely die."

Right here, we need to pause and contemplate death. How do we understand the pronouncement of death in Eden? Seeing as how death was unknown to Adam and Eve, how might they have thought of it as a deterrent for disobedience? In our time, if we commit a capital crime, we may get the death penalty.

Knowing that penalty, in some cases, can serve as a deterrent from doing the crime in the first place. It is a deterrent, though, only insofar as we both value life and fear death. Either way, to be deterred from crime, the threat of death is magnified with the lens of experience with death and life. However, Adam and Eve did not have that same experience, for they lived in a world with no, at least human, death. When God said, "In the day that you eat of it you shall surely die," how do you suppose they understood that seeing as how they lacked the same experience of death as us?

For us, we normally think of death as the time when life ends, and our bodies are no longer animated with the breath of life. Additionally, we sometimes use death to describe a spiritual condition where there remains no spiritual life in us and, although physically alive, we are dead spiritually speaking. In either case, we may reduce the definition of death to an absence of life. In the case of Adam and Eve, seeing as how they had no experience of death, the only way they could have understood death is that it meant to be absent from life. This way of thinking works if we understand their communion with God as life itself. Indeed, God is life itself; God is what it means to be. When He revealed himself to Moses, He revealed himself as being itself; "I am who I am." Being, or life, is never contingent with God. He doesn't say I was, or I will be, but I am. At all times, he is true life.

Fellowship with life itself in the garden was given in the context of a meal, the tree of life of which they

5. Sir, Have You Heard the Gospel?

could freely eat. The fruit of this tree, whether it was a real tree or a metaphor for communion with God, is no matter here, served as the basis for a sustained experience of life so long as they observed a fast from a certain tree of knowledge. To be sure, communion with God is often depicted with the image of sharing a meal.[50] However, eating from a certain forbidden tree would mean an end to this life (read, here, communion with God) they enjoyed. Yet the serpent, in his guile, suggested that they did not understand what it meant to die – that is, to have communion with life cut off.

The serpent's suggestion is quite simple. Dying, or being separated from life, (read here God) is not that bad "For God knows that when you eat of it your eyes will be opened, and you will be like God, knowing good and evil."[51] He is suggesting here that if they were to chase the things that look good (Gen. 3:6), they won't even need communion with God because they'd be like him. The serpent is suggesting that humanity just may not need to share in God's life if we were to somehow become God for ourselves. It's the same story as the tower of Babel; people try to build a tower up to heaven, and meanwhile, God has come down to inspect.[52] In our ascent, we miss His descent. To be sure, the serpent's story has never really changed.

---

50 For example, the Exodus, the giving of the Law, the Lord's Supper, the Lamb's Wedding feast, just to name a few.
51 Gen. 3:5.
52 Genesis 11:1-5

More than just suggesting a different reading of God's word by adding the word "not" to the phrase "you shall surely die," the serpent suggested that perhaps they wouldn't need fellowship with life itself if they actually *became* life (e.g., you will be like God). In other words, the serpent's narrative is a story that says, to enjoy real life, God does not need to be a part of it. This story is more complex than a tale about the fate of humanity hinged upon a question of obedience to God's law – eat this but not that. It is the origin story of our human condition; we have bought into the suggestion that what looks good, seems good, and feels right will be real life for us. Pascal was on to something!

Of course, we know that the decision of our ancestors did not make them like God, nor did it give them real life. To be sure, that decision, like all our bad decisions, provided a drop of pleasure and raging river of regret. The serpent had lied to them. Sadly, in this new condition, humanity could not just return to life itself (God) as if nothing had happened; some eggs can't be unscrambled. Why? Sin, as Paul wrote in Romans 5:12, had entered the world. Sin is a more significant issue than we typically understand. We might say sin is a transgression of the law or lawlessness. (1 John 3:4) Using the definition for the word, we might say that sin is "missing the mark." Still, others might summarize sin as doing what you shouldn't and not doing what you should. Any way you cut the cake, it seems to be that sin cannot exist where there isn't a law to break. On one level, the story of Adam and Even seems to verify this; you break

5. Sir, Have You Heard the Gospel?

the law, you sin, and therefore you die. However, while sin is lawlessness for sure, it is also more than that.

Consider the following thought experiment. When was the moment that Adam and Eve sinned so causing separation from God (life)? Was it when they saw the fruit? Was it the moment they noticed that it looked good? Was it at the moment when they considered that it might taste delicious? Or was it at the moment when the serpent said, "You're not going to die – you'll be like God"? Certainly, we would not say that they had sinned yet; there is no sin in being tempted. St. James writes that "each person is tempted when he is lured and enticed by his own desire. Then desire when it has conceived gives birth to sin; and sin when it is full-grown brings forth death."[53] So, when should we say that "desire conceived?" Was it as they reached for the fruit? Was it as they picked it? Was it as they bit into it? Was it as they chewed it? Was it as they swallowed? Was it when they enjoyed it? Now it seems as if we're on the other side of sin, doesn't it? Surely desire gave birth to sin well before they started chewing on that fruit.

Finding the moment that sin occurred is a difficult thing and surely harder than reciting law. Law is helpful only in retrospect as though on trial.

"Did they eat the fruit?"

"Yes"

"Case closed – they sinned."

---

53 James 1:14–15.

However, when did they sin? At what moment did their moral train derail? This is much more difficult to locate, not only for them but for any of us. This is because sin is a matter of the heart more than of law. Sometimes humans make good judges when it comes to the law, but we never make good judges of the heart. Life, death, and sin are matters of the heart. Jesus said as much in the Sermon on the Mountain.

"You have heard that it was said, 'You shall not commit adultery.' But I say to you that every one who looks at a woman lustfully has already committed adultery with her in his heart."[54]

Some will object here, suggesting that Jesus is instituting a new standard opposed to the law because of language like "you have heard it said...but *I* say..." Yet, if this is true, this puts Jesus at odds with the law – which he never was. Just before, he said:

"Think not that I have come to abolish the law and the prophets; I have come not to abolish them but to fulfill them."[55]

There is nothing in the text that should make us think that Jesus is upping the ante here concerning the law and making something new. To be honest, though, I read it like that in the past only because that's how it was preached to me with emphasis on the "I,"

"You have heard it said...."

"But *I* say to you..."

If you read it like that, it makes Jesus sound adversarial with the law, which we know he wasn't. If

---

54 Matt 5:27–28.
55 Matt 5:17.

5. Sir, Have You Heard the Gospel?

you read it without the emphatic "I" – which is not required – then Jesus begins to sound like a teacher of the law explaining what the law was all about underneath the letters. That is, it was never a tool to make one righteous or unrighteous so much as it was a tool to understand the sin in our lives. Our problem, then, is not law at all. The problem, as has always been the case, lies somewhere in the shadowy depths of our heart.

There must have been a moment in which Adam and Eve considered the options and decided on a course of action in line with the serpent's suggestions. This moment is not discoverable through legal means. As mysterious as this moment is, we know this moment all too well. We know the moment when, faced with temptation, we submit to its temporal pleasure. This is the lifelong struggle that our first ancestors brought into our existence. It is the fruit of the knowledge (e.g., experiential understanding) of good and evil. It is the egg that you can't unscramble. It is the truth you can't un-know. It is part of who we are. While we do not inherit the guilt of that error in judgment, we do live in the world created by it.

How does God react? Traditional stories, like I told earlier in the chapter, have God acting from a place of wrath and justice, punishing the error of the first couple by banishing them from his presence because of their disobedience. Those elements exist in the story, no doubt, but it isn't the whole story. Did Adam and Eve disobey? Yes. Did they die, that is, did were the removed from life itself, yes. Was this punishment? Maybe; consequence is probably a better word. I say that because while God must have been disappointed, he does not appear to be wrathful or even vengeful. There are two things that we could look to in the story and understand that God is not banishing them for their disobedience as he turns his back on them in their disgrace. First, He makes them garments of animal skins to do the job of covering them in their shame that their fig leaves failed to do.[56] This is not what you would expect from a God who is so holy that he can't even be in the presence of sin. Secondly, he removes the couple from the garden and from access to life, which necessarily begins the process of physical death. We should not look upon the immanence of death as a curse, however; death in Genesis 3 was an act of mercy.

> *"Then the Lord God said, "Behold, the man has become like one of us, knowing good and evil; and now, lest he put forth his hand and take also of the tree of life, and eat, and live for ever"— therefore the Lord God sent him forth from the garden of Eden, to till the ground from which he was taken. He drove out the man; and at the east of the garden of Eden he placed the cherubim, and a flaming sword which turned every way, to guard the way to the tree of life."*[57]

Consider the prospect of living forever with the reality of sin in our lives and our world. Consider the

---

56 Gen. 3:21
57 Gen. 3:22–24.

5. Sir, Have You Heard the Gospel?

agony of being in communion with pure life itself coupled with the presence of sin in our deepest fabric of who we are. To bring those two realities together in our person would be to bring destruction upon us. Consequently, God, in His mercy, has put an expiration date on the world created by our own corrupt choices and made a path to redemption. Thanks be to God that this sin-sick world cannot and will not stand forever. But that isn't the end of the story.

Since, in our ancestors, we lost access to life and returning to the dust from where we came looms on our horizon, we, like Pascal suggested, act with an instinct to fill that ancient longing within us with something. It is as if our existence is frozen in the loop of that moment in Eden vacillating between seeking life in the presence of God and trying to make a life by our effort. We have all reached for the forbidden fruit, and we have all tasted and seen that its promises are shallow. We all, like our ancestors, have excluded ourselves from life and subsequently live as though dead to life yet constantly search for life in the impending threat of our demise. This is the issue, the bad news, which we must set the good news against.

We fail to grasp the magnitude of the gospel because we fail to grasp the magnitude of sin. We fail to grasp the magnitude of sin because there are ways in which we think about sin that, while not being wrong, are not fully right. Furthermore, each of these half-truths has their own set of abuses which muddy the waters even more, leaving us with a withered concept of sin and, therefore, the gospel. On the one hand, people can think of sin as a legal issue. That is, we sin when we break the law. Since it is God's law, who is infinitely higher than man, the penalty for breaking the law, sinning, must be infinitely higher as well. If we operate under this definition of sin, then the primary virtue of life is obedience. This framework for understanding sin likewise has two abuses that run in different directions. To the right, we often see people who drift towards legalism and to the left, an exaggerated focus on God's grace and love sometimes to the point where sin becomes ill-defined and keeping ourselves from it becomes unimportant. Many of the churches of Christ with which I am familiar run between these two poles. It seems some can make sin out of anything, and others can't find sin in anything.

The issue, however, is much larger than finding the right balance between law and grace. Both of these poles are functions of defining sin as law-breaking. While sin is lawlessness, 1 John 3:4, it is also much more than that, in the same way, I might describe myself as a father: true, but I am also much more than that. If we define sin as mere law-breaking, and we believe that we are accountable only for the laws we break (Ezekiel. 18), then how do we account for the world as it is? Why does humanity (or even creation itself?) suffer as a result of the sins of only a few? Does it not seem like we are more connected? The sin was not just Eve's or just Adam's – it was their sin concerning guilt, and it is our sin concerning consequences. Furthermore, if God knows our ability to keep laws is suspect at best, why does he keep giving us new systems of law that we're bound to mess

5. Sir, Have You Heard the Gospel?

up? This is the continental divide, in my opinion, that sends some to focus on the law and pattern and others to emphasize the greatness of grace.

This is an unnecessary dichotomy based on an imperfect definition of sin. Instead of defining sin as lawlessness, we would do better to see sin as a disease with lawlessness as a symptom of that disease. Sin is that disease of our soul, of our life, that, like cancer, was brought into reality as told in the garden story. If it were merely a legal issue, God could, in his grace, simply look past our faults as he did the gentiles before Christ. (Acts 17:30) Sadly, you can't do that with disease; it must be healed. We are sick, that is the issue. Christ, the great physician has come with healing free for all people – that is the gospel. We are doomed under the penalty of death; that is the bad news. Christ has destroyed death by death itself and given us access to the life we lost in Eden – that is the good news. Of Christ's work, the author of Hebrews wrote:

> *"Since therefore the children share in flesh and blood, he himself likewise partook of the same nature, that through death he might destroy him who has the power of death, that is, the devil, and deliver all those who through fear of death were subject to lifelong bondage."* [58]

---

58 Heb. 2:14–15.

If lawlessness is a symptom of disobedience, then the law is the litmus test, which reveals the extent of our disease. Why does God give laws or commands at all? Is it not so that we, through our willingness to comply, might understand the extent of our disease? The law exists expressly for this purpose so that the disease of our soul might be brought to light. Of the law, Paul wrote that it was our tutor, or schoolmaster in some translations, "…until Christ came, that we might be justified by faith."[59] And so if we think about lawlessness as a symptom of sin, then perhaps we can begin to understand just how obedience is the symptom of faith. Indeed, the issues are much deeper than obedience versus disobedience, legalism versus grace, or faith versus works.

The real issue at stake here is life verse death; the disease of sin or the balm of Christ? No, Christ didn't come to *give* us a way; He *is* the way. He did not come to give us the truth; He is the truth. He is the life we lost in Eden, and when we find Him, we find Life. (John 14:6) The resurrection of Christ is the confirmation of this truth as we learn that death itself cannot contain the way, the truth, and the life. Likewise, to those in Christ, death will never prevail. If I could summarize the gospel using only one passage of Scripture, I would select John 11:25-26: "I am the resurrection and the life; he who believes in me, though he die, yet shall he live, and whoever lives and believes in me shall never die. Do you believe this?"

---

59 Gal. 3:24.

5. Sir, Have You Heard the Gospel?

The story of the gospel is more than the cross, more than the resurrection, and more than the ascension for none of those things would be possible without the incarnation of God in the flesh. In Eden, humanity moved away from God by attempting to ascend – to be like him. In Jesus, God descended to humanity, healed humanity, and restored life to us all. We do not need to ascend to God, for he already descended to us in Jesus. As has so often been the case, preaching the gospel as God's simple plan to forgive our sins and give us a home in heaven for eternity is not so much wrong as it is not the whole story. The gospel is a Man more than a plan. When we water the story down and tell the gospel story as just a way to manage our sins, secure some ethereal hope in the world to come, and live a better life while we wait, we run the risk of shelving the gospel in the great library of humanism along with other self-help philosophies. Subsequently, if we reduce the Christian faith to a philosophical approach to life – a mere worldview – then we run the ship aground among the reefs of pluralism being just one of the many "ways" to a better life. Indeed, the serpent's narrative in Eden was an approach to a better life. In truth, though, the gospel is the story of God descending to man so that man might ascend to God, and the goal is far more than a mere better quality of life; it is finding life itself. If we fail to articulate this gospel with precision and grace, we run the risk of counterfeiting the whole enterprise.

6.
A Reason to Die, but No Reason to Live

Honesty is always the best policy, right? Well, here it goes. As more and more of these eye-opening experiences happened, I became increasingly despondent about the entire enterprise. Instead of Christlikeness, cynicism grew in its place. Instead of grace, peace, and mercy, there was negativity, pessimism, and disinterest. I knew what I had been taught, I knew how to articulate both our position and the positions of our opponents, and I knew how to get an "AMEN!" from the back row. But what I never understood what the point of the whole thing. Why should we even go to church? Why preach, why sing, why pray? What's the whole point in living a Christian life or even life in general?

Working in the framework that I did, the gospel was a message of dealing with my sin and, subsequently, once my sin was dealt with, only heaven was left on the horizon. So much preaching about heaven was feel-good messages about how happy and sin-free we would be, and everything would be perfect. All this was hinged, of course, on your lifestyle. You may have "obeyed the gospel," and you may be "a member of the church," but if you weren't living right, it all meant nothing. So, I reasoned, and I wager that many of my brothers and sisters reasoned this way too, that the point of Christian living was merely to secure your baptismal inheritance — the premium you pay each day for the hope of heaven.

We were never able to lean too close to eternal security for fear of sounding Baptist. We distanced ourselves from faith alone lest we sound too Reformed. We would never come right out and say salvation was a product of works lest we run against the Scriptures, but, at times, it came dangerously close to that. There were always great illustrations that you would hear to make sense of those passages, but at the end of the day, it came down to a story like this. "True! We are saved by faith, but a faith that doesn't work is dead! So go ahead and say you're saved by faith, but make sure it's an active faith for an inactive faith won't save!"

Now, in a way, I don't find fault with this. But at the time, this was our hedge against the more liberal branches of the churches of Christ around us that were preaching salvation by grace in messages of love, acceptance, and tolerance. These were our brethren who fell on the other side of the silence issue

6. A Reason to Die, but No Reason to Live

and, to be sure, were not even counted as brethren in some conservative circles of my experience.

But take a moment and look at the argument a little more broadly. Regardless of how one took the silence issue, the relationship of faith and works, and the role of grace in the process of salvation (read here conservative or liberal — it doesn't matter now), these contexts were plagued with the same lurking problem. If Christian living is merely a means of demonstrating my faith to prove my love to God so that I can secure my home in heaven when this life is over, then we, by necessity, cheapen the entire enterprise of living in and of itself. I mean, what's the point in living if I'm guaranteed to sin every day and have to keep it at a distance with faithful living? Wouldn't we be better off to die right after baptism? If not, why not?

If heaven is the goal, and to go to heaven, I have to be baptized and be faithful, it makes sense, from a pragmatic perspective, to delay that for as long as possible to make my chances more secure. (If you can even apply laws of probability to this situation) I'm not the first one to think this either. Many Christians of the first few hundred years of Christian history delayed baptism for this very reason. I mean, if, like me, one was to be baptized at a young age in relative immaturity, there is a very high (read 100%) chance that you're going to sin greatly and mess that status with God up. True, there is always repentance, but what about those 11th-hour workers? They didn't work the whole day long and still got the same reward as those who did work all day. Isn't that the best use of our time? We could do whatever we wanted and enjoy life, and later in life, when our time was spent, we could be baptized and live out the short time of life following all the rules. I mean, it's the same reward either way, right? If Christian living is to be understood as an insurance premium paid on a future reward, doesn't it makes sense to pay the premium for a shorter time?

If one were so bold to make this argument (I only heard it once in 30 years, and he was laughed out of the church), preachers and teachers would have one of several retorts. The most probable response had to do with worship and fellowship. They would argue, "What about all those years of worship you're missing out on? What about all those years of fellowship? Don't you know that you have to give glory to God for all he's done for you?" True. But, at least in my contexts, the whole worship card was never dealt in the required deck. It was something that you must do according to the pattern, for sure, but was it a requirement for heaven? Not that I ever heard. So, again, why worship? Why be honest? What is the reason for not being greedy? What purpose is there in keeping your mind pure? Why refrain from gossip? What benefit is there in living with integrity, loving your neighbor, and following the golden rule, if I could just do all that at the end of my life and get the same reward? What is the purpose of life anyway?

This whole thought was exacerbated even more by the oft-repeated teaching concerning the end of time. In my context, we never focused much on the end-time theories that became so popular in the last

6. A Reason to Die, but No Reason to Live

part of the 20th century. Instead of dealing with teaching about the millennial kingdom, the rapture, and Armageddon, I most frequently heard and taught a simpler version that sidestepped all the complications. That teaching was essentially this; Jesus is coming back, the earth will be burned up, and heaven starts for some, but Hell starts for others. Simple enough, that is, unless you are struggling with finding the purpose of life in the first place. This teaching underscores the meaninglessness of life because no matter what you do, it's going to burn up anyway! And so, it boiled down to the previous issue that's solved with a simple maxim; it's all about going to heaven. If I've heard that once, I heard it a million times; it's all about going to heaven. The trouble is, I could do that just as good at the end of life as I could at the moment. The only foil to this logic is the untimely death story. If you were going to be an effective preacher, you had to have an untimely death story to encourage action in the present moment.

Untimely death stories aside, I always suspected that this thought plagued more church members than would admit to it. If I'm right here, then it probably hurt the evangelistic efforts of many would-be gospel propagators. At the time, I know it hurt mine because deep down, I just couldn't believe the story I was preaching. I mean, I'm preaching a story about a God that won't look at you because your ugly sins are in the way. The solution for this, if you ever wanted God to see you, is to interpret the Bible like me and follow the rules that don't always make sense are not consistent, as evidenced in our brotherhood. Also, if that wasn't tempting enough, acceptance of this story is not pressing because one could do it later and get the same result unless touched by an untimely death story. Oh, and if you accept it, hang on tight because it's a long ride to death. I guess you could bide your time with some good deeds or something, but everything will be burned up one day it won't matter in heaven in the least. And this is good news?

There was always one solution to the difficulties of this logic and it lay somewhere in the realm of varying degrees of reward in heaven. Preachers, not many, but some, would use that as a means to give some meaning to life, for they could add more and more to their heavenly reward. This teaching, in my experience, was never widely talked about or entertained in class settings. I'm not sure why that was, but I suspect it was due to one of two factors. First was the readiness of some to be disinterested in the teaching because, to many, heaven was heaven — shack or mansion, it didn't matter to many. Lastly, this teaching tended to open the door to questions about the partiality of God and the respect of different works. Do different works yield different rewards? Which ones are the best? As I've shown before, there were not many willing to journey into these weeds or any weeds for that matter, and the debate usually died there.

When I read The Acts of the Apostles, though, I met men and women who died for what they believed in, and there I sat searching for a reason to live for what I believed; how backward is that? The Apostles and Martyrs, through the years, had such pro-

6. A Reason to Die, but No Reason to Live

found faith in the risen Lord that they gladly accepted death as a natural part of living the life of their crucified Lord. I knew something was wrong with my approach, for I didn't have faith like them; they gladly accepted death, and I couldn't even find a reason to gladly accept life! My faith honestly wasn't faith at all. Looking back on it now, I see that it was more philosophy with Christian labels than a life based on faith. I say philosophy because conversions were won in arguments, not experiences. Leaders were chosen for their ideas, not their actions. Preachers were scheduled for their charismatic speaking, not for the image of God that they bore on their souls. Jesus was always held up as the master teacher more than the Son of God, and we were faithful to his ideas, not necessarily to Him the person. He taught us a better way, like a philosopher might, with wisdom from above, which he had access to by his sonship.

There are some in the churches of Christ who, although they may be unaware, fully affirm this position and suppose that the purpose of life is to study, worship, pray, and grow in wisdom and knowledge every day. I've heard that proposed from many pulpits. That's not a terrible goal in and of itself, however. Surely there is nothing wrong with wanting to be more informed and wise (that is unless what you learn goes against tradition, then you might be advised to stay away from that). Unfortunately, even this doesn't solve the case of the missing purpose in life because what will it amount to in the end? Even the best of our knowledge is imperfect and will pass away. (1 Cor. 13:8-9) If Christianity couldn't provide any real meaning to living aside from preparing to die, could anything give life meaning?

Generations of people smarter than I have tried to get at the meaning of life. Some, assuming we are essentially animalistic, suppose that our purpose is merely to procreate and survive and that survival is reserved for the fittest among us. Some push back against the survival instinct and encourage humans to thrive in their lives, working for more than mere existence. In our individualistic society, many suggest that life's purpose is merely whatever makes you happy, and we all chase personal meaning and truth in our unique ways. I used to have a shirt that said, "He who dies with the most toys wins." How foolish. If we are all entitled to our ideas, then equally valid is the idea that life has no intrinsic meaning at all.

In popular Christian estimation, however, people tend to recoil from individualistic and nihilistic interpretations of purpose. Rather, preachers and teachers tend to suggest that our purpose is found in worshipping and enjoying God and living life according to His purpose, which he revealed to us in Christ. This notion is propped up, usually, with the thought that everything was made for the glory of God and that until we realize that and give glory where glory is due, we will be operating outside the bounds of our God-given purpose. I don't want to rewrite Rick Warren's popular *Purpose Driven Life* here, nor do I want to critique it, but this is essentially what many Christian teachers and preachers would submit to us, albeit not as charismatically. To narrow the field somewhat, the most common purpose of life story

6. A Reason to Die, but No Reason to Live

that I heard in the churches of Christ revolved around worship. I was told, from the pulpit, "You were made to worship God!"

What is the real purpose of life? Is it worship? Is it finding God's plan for my life and living out His mandates? Why did God create us, and what does he want from us? To be sure, this is neither a simple existential question nor existentially simple. While this may not be the best place for a deep excursion into questions and proofs concerning God's existence, I do want to pause for a moment and offer a brief apology as to why I think our true purpose must be found in God. If you're still reading this book, you probably don't doubt God's existence, and neither do you dismiss the thought that we indeed have a purpose somehow related to God. If you happen to find yourself doubting His existence now, or debating whether or not we even have a purpose, you may find my reasoning a little disappointing as I am assuming the existence of both. Assuming both, then, why should we find our purpose in God?

What do we mean when we say "purpose?" Consider a hammer; what is its purpose? Of course, the hammer exists to drive nails into building materials. This is one sense of the meaning of purpose. It follows, then, that to find our purpose in life means to find what we are made to do or what role we are to fill. In this way of thinking, we are workers trying to find our niche. From a different perspective, though, we still haven't addressed the fullness of the hammer's purpose. To get at that, we must learn to see the hammer through a broader lens, widening our scope from its beginning to its end. Given any random hammer, we know that it didn't always exist, and one day it won't exist anymore. Even if we, like Plato, moved from the image of a hammer to the abstract idea of the hammer we would not yet find anything necessary to existence itself. If we suddenly lost the idea of a hammer, the world would still turn, and the sun would still rise. Ultimately, then, hammers are unimportant and meaningless because, while they drive nails, they do not serve an eternal purpose.

It seems to me that for any purpose to be a real, meaningful purpose, it must be an eternal purpose. In the classical sense, then, this is God; God is the eternal purpose *par excellence*. This is because if something had a beginning, then it cannot be absolutely necessary to creating life, and if it had an end, it is not necessary to sustain life. This is the trap of humanity's quest for purpose. We have a beginning, and we have an end and, while we may drive nails, we struggle with finding an eternal purpose. And so it follows, then, that if we are going to find our eternal purpose and have a real, meaningful life, then it must be found in *the* eternal purpose which is God himself for there is no other eternal. Or, as the preacher of Ecclesiastes says, "He has made everything beautiful in its time; also he has put eternity into man's mind, yet so that he cannot find out what God has done from the beginning to the end."[60] Any purpose or meaning that we may ascribe to life, if it is not eternal by nature, will ultimately pass away and be ultimately

---

60 Eccl. 3:11.

6. A Reason to Die, but No Reason to Live

meaningless. In sum, if real meaning in life is eternal, and we find eternity in God, then real meaning in life is found in God.

Again, if you're still reading this, you probably won't argue with the idea that our meaning in life must be grounded in the eternal if the meaning we ascribe to life is to be authentic. As I wrote before in an earlier chapter, even though we may agree in principle with this, it can still be difficult to truly grasp this meaning and build a meaningful life therein. I say this pointing the finger squarely at myself. As before, I was preaching, teaching, and living the outward form of a Christian way of life as it was handed down to me, yet I still failed to see the purpose in all of it; I know I'm not the only one. Many, including myself, affirmed that meaning was found in God — in the eternal — but that it was only realized in the world to come. Following that, we would say that the purpose of life is to get to heaven, wherein we find our real life. However, if we say that the purpose of life is simply "getting to heaven," we haven't helped shape life's trajectory at all. If heaven is the all-important goal, and this life is just a means to that end, then life is nothing more than a journey to be endured, and it doesn't explain why God put us here if He's only interested in what comes next. In this estimation, life has no real value because it functions as a sort of scaffolding until we get to heaven. Once the goal of heaven is reached, the scaffolding can be torn down and done away with. Can life mean more? I think it can, and I think it does. Now, I want to explore what I hinted at before, namely, that this way of thinking can diminish our life instead of actualizing it as it obscures life's true purpose for us altogether. As before, the story begins in Eden.

Why did God create man? I hesitate to even field an answer here. Who am I to presume to know the mind of God? Yet, I feel as though I need to at least propose an answer if for no other reason than to offer an alternative to the reasons so often presented. That often presented reason has to do with worship. It may not be the case for you, but I've nearly always heard that we were made to worship and give glory to God and that we exist for his praise. A preacher once told me that when we reach our goal of heaven, we'll be eternally worshipping God, so you better enjoy worship now because you're going to be doing a lot of it in the world to come! To be clear, though, he figured we'd all be singing four part harmony Stamps-Baxter music all through the sweet by and by. He even went so far as to say that if we didn't enjoy worship now, then we wouldn't enjoy heaven either. Essentially, so the story went, humanity was made to worship God, they will eternally worship God, and if they don't, they will be destroyed in Hell.

I don't need to tell you how horrible this idea sounds. To me, and frankly many critics, this idea makes God seem narcissistic because it supposes God to have created man simply to shower him with eternal praise. It makes me think about God as though he needed praise and is not complete without our melodies and prayers ascending to His ears. If this is the case, is this even a God worthy of our worship, seeing as how he lacks something? Furthermore, how

6. A Reason to Die, but No Reason to Live

does knowing that our only point in life is to worship an insatiable being give any value to life? I am not suggesting here that worship is not important. I am not even suggesting that worship isn't an essential element of the Christian life. I am, however, rejecting the idea that worship is the fundamental purpose in living and that supposing it is can drive many people away from considering the great value of faith altogether.

As I wrote before in the chapter on the gospel, understanding life and death is a necessary prerequisite for understanding the gospel. It turns out that it is also helpful in understanding our purpose. This should make sense, right? Knowing the purpose of life is a hard puzzle to solve if we don't know what life is in the first place. Without rewriting that chapter, remember that God is life, and he shares that life in union with his creation. Adam and Eve had life when they enjoyed their fellowship with God in the garden before that fateful fruit. After they ate, they lost their lives for they lost their union. The life they lost was not physical (bios) — although that followed — but spiritual life, which was union with God. God is life. Jesus, God in the flesh, affirmed as much in John 14:6.

If God is true life, then any life lived outside of God is not real life at all, and while it may have a temporal purpose, it has no eternal purpose. Remember the hammer illustration? How then, do we get our temporal life with its temporal purpose to become eternal life with eternal purpose? Is it not an exercise in reestablishing the union of God and man?

Yet, this union of God and man is *the* man Jesus who, coincidently, offers eternal life through faith in Him. (John 3:16) It follows, then, that to know life is to know God, and if I do not know God, I do not know life. I may know some version of life, some shadow of life, but life in its true will remain hidden.

Eternal life is more than just life without an end. I know I grew up thinking that eternal life simply meant that you didn't die anymore and that somehow this was our prize because "God so loved the world." But eternal doesn't mean "no end" to the exclusion of all else, far from it. We must remember that eternal, if it is truly eternal, has no beginning or end. What is this eternal life, then? Eternal life is a way to describe *the* life — God himself. Jesus does not talk about this life as some life we enjoy later on after we die. Rather, it is our participation in *the* life right now. In this way, eternal life is enjoyed both now *and* in the age to come. Notice the use of present tense verbs (in bold) in John 3.

> *"No one has ascended into heaven but he who descended from heaven, the Son of man. And as Moses lifted up the serpent in the wilderness, so must the Son of man be lifted up, that whoever **believes** in him may have eternal life. For God so loved the world that he gave his only Son, that whoever **believes** in him should not perish but have eternal life. For God sent the Son into the world, not*

6. A Reason to Die, but No Reason to Live

> *to condemn the world, but that the world might be saved through him."*[61]

This "life in the present" thinking is all through John. (John 3:36; 4:14; 5:24; 6:47; 10:28) This is to say that whoever is believing in Christ *has* eternal life. Does this mean we do not die or that we are never born? Of course not! But it does mean that through faith (e.g., born anew, or born from above, or born again), we begin to share in *the* life that is without beginning or end — God Himself. Thus, life, our physical and spiritual existence, is about participation in God in the present age, and this life will not end with our death. Again, this life that he speaks about is not physical at all but rather spiritual. "Truly, truly, I say to you, if anyone keeps my word, he will never see death."[62]

He's clearly not talking about biological life here as both He and his followers all died a physical death. But, by the resurrection of Jesus, we have the truth of His life confirmed. Yes, he died physically, but not spiritually. And this life that was in Him was *the* life, and although it validated him and His ministry, it also changed him physically in the resurrection. It is the reversal of Eden. There, Adam and Eve lost spiritual life, and it ultimately changed them physically so that the flesh was an image of what had happened spiritually — death. But Christ *is* spiritual life, and, although he died, his physical life was changed into the image of glory instead of the image of corruption.

---

61 John 3:13–17.
62 John 8:51.

All this is to say that to know real life is to know eternal life, and eternal life is not something reserved for the future. Eternal life, the life of God, can be enjoyed now, and to know life is to know God. Jesus said,

> *"Father, the hour has come; glorify thy Son that the Son may glorify thee, since thou hast given him power over all flesh, to give eternal life to all whom thou hast given him. And this is eternal life, that they know thee the only true God, and Jesus Christ whom thou hast sent."*[63]

To know God in Jesus Christ is life itself, and knowing God is the purpose of life. The Law, or any law for matter, cannot save us because through it, we cannot know God. Sure, we can know things about God, what he may like or dislike, but we fail to know him experientially. Good living, morality, service, worship, and things like these cannot save us for the same reason. To be sure, worship, morality, service, and such like are all part of the Christian life, but they are not an end unto themselves. That is, we do not exist for them; rather, they exist for us so that through them, we may come to know God who is life. Maximus the Confessor (7th Century) is famously quoted as saying that truth does not exist for virtue, but rather virtue exists for truth. In other words, we do not learn the truth so that we can live good upstanding moral lives being the best employee, parent, child,

---

[63] John 7:1–3, emphasis mine.

6. A Reason to Die, but No Reason to Live

or neighbor we can be; it's actually the opposite. We live good moral, upstanding lives, we worship, we study, and we love our neighbor *so that we might* come to know God through them and experience real life (eternal life). God did not give the law to the Jews so that they would be the most well-behaved people on earth; he gave the Law so that they might know Him, the Lord of all creation.[64]

Christianity, then, cannot be a mere philosophy or rule of life. Rather, it is the "way" in which we come to know God, and that way is Christ (John 14:6). Strictly speaking, nothing else will do here: no other person, no other idea, no other action, and no other philosophy. This is because Christ is the image of God himself. (Col. 1:15) Of Christ, the Hebrew author wrote that "He reflects the glory of God and bears the very stamp of his nature, upholding the universe by his word of power."[65] Jesus is the radiance of God's glory, the image of His person, the Word of God, and Immanuel — God with us. He is the joining of human and divine life and the crowing of human hope. Every other philosophy, religion, or principle of life starts with some supposed truth that leads to some virtue that is mistaken for real life. But in Christ, we begin with life itself — God being joined to human nature in the incarnation — and we live this life (relationships, morality, worship, etc.) using all these associated virtues to grow in our knowledge (read relational and experiential) of God. Thus, the goal and purpose of human life, far from simply "getting to

---

64 Ex. 29:45-46
65 Heb. 1:3.

heaven" is to know God in Jesus Christ. To know Him is to love Him for God is love.

I realize, however, that this does not yet answer the question about why God made man in the first place. If we reject the idea that God made us so that we might worship him, what do we replace it with? Is it better to think that God made us so that we might know him? Why human life? Why not angles? Could angelic powers not also know God? If so, could they not know him more completely? After all, aren't angels supposed to be eternal spirit beings like God? How does human life provide any advantage to knowing God?

We face a host of issues that angels do not seem to struggle with. We hunger, and we thirst, and we battle the temptations of darkness. We grow old, we break, we deteriorate, and we die. We are weak, of limited intelligence, and have a capacity for selfishness and evil. Humanity doesn't seem to have a great resume, does it? Did God know all this when he made man? He must have, we suppose, else he is not the omniscient God we suspect Him to be. We have a decision to make. Either a) God didn't see the fall coming, and it surprised him, b) God suspected the fall might occur and was prepared for it, or c) He knew it was a certainty and is okay with it. If we choose either of the first two options, then we have to deal with God in our theology that does not know with 100% certainty what might happen tomorrow. We'll reject those for now — that version of God is hardly a god at all. What we are left with is a theology that suggests God knew the fall was a certainty yet

6. A Reason to Die, but No Reason to Live

went ahead and created man in the garden with a choice anyway. This is more than the establishment of free will though it is that for sure. If we are to love God, then we have to choose to love God, and we can't do that without a choice; this is the truth but not the whole truth.

As I've been getting at, God had to have known what Adam and Eve would choose and that it would eventually lead to their separating and death. This has to mean, then, that this mortal existence that is "a little lower than the angels" is the reality that God saw when he breathed life into the nostrils of man. He must have seen the suffering and the pain we would endure. He must have seen the tears we would shed when we lose loved ones. He must have seen the terror and destruction caused by sin and lawlessness. And despite all this, he still created us and allowed us to live in its midst. That must mean there is something special about this human experience and that suffering together with death gives us an advantage that no angel could hope for. Many atheists reject the possibility of God's existence precisely for this "problem of evil." Instead, it is this "problem" that is actually humanity's distinct advantage over all other created life in Heaven and on Earth.

How could suffering and death equip us to know God when God neither suffers nor dies? This is the problem that all other world religions must wrestle with save Christianity for our God, in Christ, both suffered and died just like us. God is perfectly revealed to us in Jesus, and Jesus showed us divinity by humility, weakness, limitation, suffering, and death. Paul put it like this:

> *"Have this mind among yourselves, which is yours in Christ Jesus, who, though he was in the form of God, did not count equality with God a thing to be grasped, but emptied himself, taking the form of a servant, being born in the likeness of men. And being found in human form he humbled himself and became obedient unto death, even death on a cross. Therefore God has highly exalted him and bestowed on him the name which is above every name, that at the name of Jesus every knee should bow, in heaven and on earth and under the earth, and every tongue confess that Jesus Christ is Lord, to the glory of God the Father."*[66]

This kenotic self-humiliation is not possible in angelic life. Only mortality and weakness can grasp this indefinable quality of God's person. Far from running from suffering and death, we should embrace it as did our savior not with a victim mentality to win points with God but so that through our patient endurance, we might come to know God as he is. Knowing God is the goal and purpose of life, and there is no arena better than this mortal existence. God did not come to us in angelic form; he came to us as a man. The first two chapters of Hebrews bear truth perfectly.

---

66 Php. 2:5–11.

6. A Reason to Die, but No Reason to Live

> *"For to what angel did God ever say, "Thou art my Son, today I have begotten thee"? Or again, "I will be to him a father, and he shall be to me a son"? And again, when he brings the first-born into the world, he says, "Let all God's angels worship him." Of the angels he says, "Who makes his angels winds, and his servants flames of fire." But of the Son he says, "Thy throne, O God, is for ever and ever, the righteous scepter is the scepter of thy kingdom."*[67]

Notice the contrast in glory between the incarnate Son of God and the angelic powers. More than just a discourse of the supremacy of Christ, this is a discourse on how people approach God. On one side, what we might call the angelic approach, people try to approach God by service; this is what they suppose they were made to do. On the other side, the approach to God is through a relationship — Father/Son, specifically in this case. This relationship, this intimate knowledge enjoyed in Christ, is far superior to mere obedience because it is a knowledge learned through obedient suffering and death.

> *"Now in putting everything in subjection to him, he left nothing outside his control. As it is, we do not yet see everything in subjection to him. But we see Jesus, who for a little while was made lower than the angels, crowned with glory and honor because of the*

---

67 Heb. 1:5–8.

suffering of death, so that by the grace of God he might taste death for every one. For it was fitting that he, for whom and by whom all things exist, in bringing many sons to glory, should make the pioneer of their salvation perfect through suffering. For he who sanctifies and those who are sanctified have all one origin. That is why he is not ashamed to call them brethren, saying, "I will proclaim thy name to my brethren, in the midst of the congregation I will praise thee." And again, "I will put my trust in him." And again, "Here am I, and the children God has given me." Since therefore the children share in flesh and blood, he himself likewise partook of the same nature, that through death he might destroy him who has the power of death, that is, the devil, and deliver all those who through fear of death were subject to lifelong bondage. For surely it is not with angels that he is concerned but with the descendants of Abraham. Therefore he had to be made like his brethren in every respect, so that he might become a merciful and faithful high priest in the service of God, to make expiation for the sins of the people. For because he himself has suffered and been tempted, he is able to help those who are tempted."[68]

The advantage of humanity is, paradoxically, our weakness. We can learn to live because we die. We can learn to appreciate and long for the good because of our tendency toward darkness and evil; this is the

---

68 Hebrews 2:8–18, emphasis mine.

6. A Reason to Die, but No Reason to Live

knowledge of good and evil. We can know the light as it shines into the darkness. In this construction, this is why God allows suffering and hardships in our life. It is not a detriment to our survival; it is our means of life. Paul prayed thus about his "thorn in the flesh," and God didn't remove it. Again, contrary to reason, instead of removing his sorrow, God allowed it to remain. But for what purpose? Is it not to allow Paul to know the grace of Christ?

> *"Three times I besought the Lord about this, that it should leave me; but he said to me, "My grace is sufficient for you, for my power is made perfect in weakness." I will all the more gladly boast of my weaknesses, that the power of Christ may rest upon me. For the sake of Christ, then, I am content with weaknesses, insults, hardships, persecutions, and calamities; for when I am weak, then I am strong."* [69]

Human life is so much more than worship and service; this is the role of the angelic powers. Ours is to know God relationally, experientially, and intimately. This knowledge, however, can only be acquired in the realm of mortality for here we learn what it means to sacrifice, to love, to lose, to suffer, to wait, to endure, to triumph, and to fail. Because of the cross, we know that suffering does not impede man's access to God;

---

[69] 2 Cor. 12:8–10.

instead, it is the means of knowing God in his fullness.

This changes, or it should at least, how we approach every single aspect of our lives. Instead of Christian faith giving us principles that make us better spouses, parents, children, employees, employers, servants, or rulers, Christian faith actually gives each of these aspects new meaning in that they become ways in which to know and experience God. Popular approaches suppose that humanity has a list of affections, and God should be at the top followed closely by family, then other responsibilities, then yourself last. A folksy way you may have seen it presented is using the acronym J.O.Y; Jesus first, others next, yourself last. What I am arguing in this construction, however, is that there is no list at all — just God. God is number one, and there is no two through whatever. Knowing this God in Jesus is all that matters, and every relationship is more than a simple opportunity to apply Christian principles; it is, in reality, an opportunity to deepen *the* relationship.

Take the marriage relationship, for example. On the one hand, people say husbands must love your wives and treat them with respect for the Bible commands it, yet, you still have to love God more than your spouse. While there is a kernel of truth to that, on the other hand, what I am presenting goes something like this. One might say, I love God, and the marriage relationship is a way for me to come to know God, especially his relationship to the Church in Jesus. Consequently, being faithful in your marriage is, in reality, being faithful to the Lord Himself

6. A Reason to Die, but No Reason to Live

and loving your spouse, your children, or even your neighbor is a way in which you demonstrate your increasing knowledge of God in love. Thinking in this way invigorates all our relationships with others since they now become avenues in which we perfect our knowledge of God. This is exactly why we are taught to love our enemy so that we might come to know how God in Christ loved us "while we were yet enemies."[70] Knowing God, not mere obedience to a law, is the ultimate reason and motive behind every action. We worship God to know him not to appease him. We pray so that we might know Him not so that he will grant our wishes. We serve others, the poor, our neighbor, and the marginalized to know God because that is what God in Christ has done for us who are poor and marginalized in spirit.

What do we discover when we come to know God? You might also ask what do you discover when you come to know a spouse or a close friend. Learning facts is only part of the story and not even a helpful fragment at that. If a husband were to know all the facts about his wife, it would not come close to replacing the experiential knowledge gained by a close and intimate relationship. Knowing what someone is thinking is not the same thing as being able to finish one another's sentences. Knowing people is not something you can learn in a book; how much more, then, is this true for the infinite God? Yes, we need the Bible, we need worship, we need service, we need nature, we need all these things, but none of them

---

70 Rom. 5:10

replace years of dedicated experience and loyalty tempered with unceasing prayer. In this, then, we will find the value of life — it is our context to experience and to know God. Could you be saved if you waited until the end of your life? Well, if by that you mean simply going to heaven when you die the yes. But salvation is so much more than that. Salvation is *true* life and the experience of true life right now. Salvation is coming to experience the life of God in Christ by the power of the Holy Spirit within us. This is a reason to get up every morning and love my neighbor because in some way, God lives in that interaction. There is no reason to delay this, seeing as how this is real life. Every other quest is a waste of time.

I want to wrap this chapter up by making one final plea concerning Christian distinction and what makes Christian faith different from all the other approaches to divine knowledge. I do not want to reinvent the wheel here, nor do I want to stray from my purpose, but one final thing is worth mentioning, and that concerns the nature of God. If you take the Bible all by itself, *sola scriptura*, you may or may not end up connecting some very important dots concerning the nature of God. I say this because, in the course of Christian history, it took several hundred years to condense, distill, and formalize the doctrine of the Trinity and the nature of Christ's relationship to human nature. If one ignores church history and the greater context of Scripture, they'd be lucky to make the same connections that it took many other faithful souls centuries to condense. Yet, these are vital dots to connect and a truth for which people through the

6. A Reason to Die, but No Reason to Live

ages have fought and died. Christian faith is not so much faith with a Trinitarian aspect as it is faith *in* the Trinitarian God. When we stand at a distance from the fathers of the church and refuse to rely on their collective wisdom, we do our search for deeper and more complete truth a great disservice. Through the years, they have fought valiantly to protect the truth of the nature of our God revealed in Jesus and insisted that this God is three persons, each of whom is fully God, yet there is only one God.

In the churches of Christ with which I am familiar, the Trinitarian doctrine was never stressed. It was more like an interesting tidbit of faith trivia that we kept on the shelf and dusted off from time to time, for, as I was told, the word "Trinity" is not in the Bible. However, after years of study and reflection, I've come to realize that if God is a Trinity of Persons and knowing that God is the purpose of life, then knowing God and experiencing God *as* Trinity is the foundation to Christian practice, not something you pull out from time to time as a matter of doctrinal alignment. This is a strong statement but there no getting around it. This is not the place for a defense of classical definitions of the Trinity, but it is a good place to encourage you to spend some time with this topic. It's important because if we don't worship the God who is Father, Son, and Hoy Spirit, who is confessed as such by the church for two millennia, then we are not worshipping the God of the Bible. Furthermore, if we are attempting to know God and ignore this Trinitarian nature, we will never flourish. Without a communion of persons in Trinity, there is no communion at all, there is no real fellowship, and there is no real love or life. Without the Father who is in the Son and the Son who is in the Father by the presence of the Holy Spirit, there is no way for any of us to be "in Christ." Without the God who is "Father of all, above all, through all, and in all" (Eph. 4:6) who "has sent his Son as the Savior of the world" (1 John 4:14) there is no way to "abide in Christ." (John 15) However, because of God existing eternally as Father, Son, and Holy Spirit (The Trinity — a communion of persons) we can experientially and intimately know God. Perhaps there is not a better way to conclude than with the words of St. John.

"Beloved, let us love one another; for love is of God, and he who loves is born of God and knows God. He who does not love does not know God; for God is love. In this the love of God was made manifest among us, that God sent his only Son into the world, so that we might live through him. In this is love, not that we loved God but that he loved us and sent his Son to be the expiation for our sins. Beloved, if God so loved us, we also ought to love one another. No man has ever seen God; if we love one another, God abides in us and his love is perfected in us. By this we know that we abide in him and he in us, because he has given us of his own Spirit. And we have seen and testify that the Father has sent his Son as the Savior of the world."[71]

---

71 1 Jn 4:7–14, emphasis mine.

7.
A Final Word?

We have come to the end of one story and the beginning of another. I have tried to illustrate how my experience growing up in the churches of Christ throughout West Virginia, opened my eyes and piqued my curiosity as I grappled with both nagging questions and inconsistencies in faith and practice. My experience, I'm willing to bet with near certainty, is not that much different from many people who grew up in similar contexts. The issues, for me anyway, boiled down essentially to questions concerning the nature of the Bible and its interpretation, what it means to be the church, and being able to speak the gospel with precision all in a manner that exposes and supports the real meaning to life. I realize these are all major foundational issues, and tussling with these titans isn't something one does overnight. As we close this narrative, I want to encourage you to wrestle with your questions, for they are worth the struggle; it can be the impetus for real growth. Let me end, then, with a few final reflections.

First, faith is worth saving. I realize that American society is by-in-large a consumer society full of consumers consuming consumables. This isn't how it's always been, though. There was a time, so I'm told, that if your TV broke, you took it to a repairman. I remember the tail end of those days. I made a trip with my father to the TV repair shop once, and I remember having our Zenith TV with the giant dial knobs on the front repaired. I can even recall having shoes repaired on that same street. Now, we just toss them out and get even better replacements. Is it not easier that way?

I suppose there is a time to toss out the things that don't work but I urge caution that we don't throw out the wrong thing. Sometimes, we must confess, it is our understanding of faith that is broken and not faith itself. When it comes to one's faith tradition, one's church, or even one's faith, how do you know if it's savable? How do you determine whether you should on one hand tinker with it, attempt some expensive repairs, and then soldier on or, on the other hand, scrap it and look for something new? F. LaGard Smith wrestled with this very question in his book *Radical Restoration*.[72]

I am not the first person, nor will I be the last, to struggle with one's faith tradition. The world is full of stories about people who either give up leaving the

---

72 F. LaGard Smith, *Radical Restoration: A Call for Pure and Simple Christianity*. (Nashville, TN: Cotswald Pub. 2001)

7. A Final Word?

faith altogether or stick it out, trying each day to make the best of it. I trust people make those decisions carefully while weighing the consequences and benefits of either pole. I think we need to trust that people do not make these decisions lightly and, instead of some accusatory stance, we should engage with these people with a goal of mutual respect and understanding. Throughout this narrative, though, I hope you have witnessed how, for me, at least, it was not faith in the Lord Jesus that was traumatizing and confusing, it was simply my approach to understanding it all.

You would think quitting altogether would simply be the easiest option. Many people experience frustration with the church and just walk away from faith altogether. I'm sure you have firsthand knowledge of many who have hiked this path. For me, at least, just tossing the whole thing out was never seemed like a viable option. Albeit, there was a particularly dark year of my life in which I didn't go to church at all. I didn't pray, I didn't study, and I lived a lifestyle that was anything but Christian. That year, as I said, was dark, and it wasn't easy at all. No, I didn't deal with the same issues I had when I was preaching and teaching in the churches, but the load was not lighter. You would think that if my real problem was with the tradition, then leaving the tradition would fix it all, but it didn't. I just changed out a series of problems for a different collection.

This was due, in part, to the fact that even though I was removed from that current at the time, I was still a product of that current and, like it or not, our traditions leave their stamps on us in ways often unimaginable. Although I knew I wasn't reading the Bible correctly, and I seemed to never be satisfied with the standard answers, I still believed the Scriptures and knew the reality to which they witnessed was true. The argument that St. Paul made in Romans 7 applies here. He wrote:

> "What then shall we say? That the law is sin? By no means! Yet, if it had not been for the law, I should not have known sin. I should not have known what it is to covet if the law had not said, "You shall not covet." But sin, finding opportunity in the commandment, wrought in me all kinds of covetousness. Apart from the law sin lies dead. I was once alive apart from the law, but when the commandment came, sin revived and I died; the very commandment which promised life proved to be death to me. For sin, finding opportunity in the commandment, deceived me and by it killed me."[73]

It was because I knew and believed what I had read in the Scriptures, that I knew there was something wrong in my life. Just taking a break from church doesn't fix anything because it's not the real problem. So in a way, if you are experiencing troubles in your faith tradition, leaving it in exchange for nothing will probably cause far more excruciating pain in the long run than you may have experienced while being a

---

73   Romans 7:7–11

7. A Final Word?

functioning member. It's as if you realize you have a broken TV and instead of repairing it or buying a new one, you just toss it out and have no TV at all! I realize this is the course that some people go, and I think it really should be the most alarming thing for folks in churches of Christ, or any church for that matter, to hear. What this is saying is that there are people who would rather go nowhere and believe nothing than continue another day in that context. This is truly sad.

Of course, there will be those atheistic voices who tell you the story about their troublesome and, at times, even abusive upbringing in their religious context, and they'll tell the story about how leaving the faith altogether was the best decision ever. I know this because I spent time talking to atheists one summer as I was working through my doubts. After a few conversations, I boiled some thoughts down to a single hypothesis; atheists appear to have no positive reason to be atheists; they are always negative. In other words, I never talked to a professed atheist who had an attraction to non-belief based on positive data or experiences. All the conversations I had featured the same reoccurring theme; they had become atheists by default when faith appeared either abusive or improbable. It seemed as if atheism was the proverbial corner in which their life experiences had painted them.

No, I am not trying to convince you that I am an experienced debater, nor am I some philosopher apologist for traditional Christian affirmations. At the lowest point in my life when I wasn't practicing any semblance of Christian faith at all, it should be noted that it wasn't philosophy and apologetics that kept me from leaping into the formless void of the atheist or otherwise unaffiliated. What brought me back to the pew was the values that the tradition itself, with all its flaws and all its shortcomings, had instilled within me. For better or for worse, warts and all, it had made me what I was. The current which I had ridden for so long was simply too strong to neglect. And so, I returned. Simple as that. I wish I had one of those movie moments to share with you that transcended all reason and thought. I wish there were a mystical experience of the divine reality that I could point to and say, "Yes, that was the moment!" There was no single moment of revelation where it all made sense. It was simply a process of conscious reflection within the current of my tradition.

I'm not so naïve to suppose that it works this way for everyone. Some people who have left altogether may need to hear sound arguments, apologetics, and see many "infallible proofs" demonstrated before them so that they can return. Surely, these stories abound in some circles too. I reasoned that if a tradition could influence a person so greatly, even from a distance, and if that tradition's influence was meant for good, then there must be something there that is worth trying to repair. In the ensuing years, I took up preaching again. I took up teaching again. This time, however, I was convinced things were going to be different. I was going to speak from the heart instead of the platform of the tradition's politics. I was going to take up the mantle yet again, search for real answers, and I was going to lead other willing minds

7. A Final Word?

and souls to a deeper and richer experience of faith than ever before. If God could bring me back — one who didn't even seem to understand the gospel at all — he could work wonders with just about anyone.

As anyone who has tried this before can attest, suggesting ideas that seem to run contrary to the status quo can land you in hot water. Perhaps that's the case in all churches. In fairness, there is a certain admirable quality in measured stubbornness. Maybe I feel that way because I don't feel bad about the extent of my stubbornness, maybe not. Still, if traditions are to survive in an ever-changing cultural context, it must have people who are committed to staying the course. However, keeping a tradition from going too far in one direction is only one side of the coin. Traditions need critics to prevent meandering in the opposite direction. These critics provide an important balance alerting the traditions to an error in a contrasting direction. Depending on your perspective, you could say that both the critic and the conservative love and serve the tradition for which they fight.

Considering the churches of Christ, I began to see myself as someone who fulfilled a critical role. Not only because of my changing views on things but because I noticed that people I most admired within my tradition were its critics. I was a critic who believed the tradition was worth saving but feared that it had drifted, as a movement in some instances, too far off the path. In my sermons and my classes, I often chipped away at these things trying to demonstrate the value of appreciating the Bible in its historical context and the rich depository of 2000 years of Christian history. All this, so I thought, would be some of the most fertile soil we've ever seen for putting down deep roots of faith. I may win some, and I may lose some along the way, but I felt like I at least trying to steer things positively. Wrong again.

The trouble is, if you shift the norm for biblical interpretation to something that is both historically accurate and intellectually defensible, you will begin to read the Bible in a new light (a historically accurate and intellectually honest light). Familiar verses will shine with new luster, and stories will reverberate with the melody of fresh wisdom. It seems so simple to say, but it's still worth saying; reading Scripture with a different lens alters the way you read it, and thinking about church in a different way changes how you see it.

As this began to happen, I saw little things here and there in the tradition that just didn't seem right anymore. To be sure, many of them were silly, and I chalked it up to me just being nit-picky. I wasn't afraid to suggest a new course on some things or thinking about the accepted norms from new perspectives. Some people met that with enthusiasm, and I always suspected that I was saying the sort of thing they were thinking but had not said for whatever reason. What I learned, though, is that it is one thing to suggest an examination of some of the more marginal ideas but quite another to tread on the fundamentals. The trick is, not everyone agrees on what those fundamentals are. To some in the churches of Christ, the fundamental of fundamentals is baptism, and it can never be subject to any scrutiny, rethinking,

7. A Final Word?

or examination. To others, it was worship issues like instrumental music or the Lord's Supper that held that untouchable status. It seems for every hill to die on there was always someone willing to volunteer as tribute.

I can safely say that I didn't take any of these issues lightly. I tried my very best to think through them without emotional attachment, simply trying to be logical and rational. At times, people in the churches of Christ were, like any church in the world, coarse and judgmental, but I tried hard not to let these experiences become my "why." I committed myself to arrive at a defensible and honest understanding of the issues mentioned above, even if it meant I had to change my views. Now, years later, after all the reading, writing, and struggle, I can safely say that absolutely none of my views or understandings changed overnight. Every single piece of the puzzle began as a mere kernel of thought that I couldn't shake away, nor could I let it rest. I believe I understand the gravity of the situation and ideas I'm suggesting, and I hope you do too. These questions fixated me, as I'm sure your questions do to you, and now, I can rest in the evening with peace, knowing that I did the work required. It took a large investment both of time and money to answer these questions. As all the dust from this quest is settling, I sit here at my desk surrounded by a mountain of books and files, a seminary degree, and a brand-new outlook on life made possible, ironically, by none of those things. I did not so much learn new dogmas as I answered the call of St. Andrew himself as he said, "Come, we have found Him for whom we yearned!"

Still, although my assessment of things has changed in many regards, my context of worship, the formational current if you will, had not. Until the spring of 2019, I was still preaching and teaching regularly for the churches of Christ. However, instead of preaching standard interpretations and applications, as I did in the past, I was preaching the gospel as I had come to understand it. I was focusing on the incarnation of Jesus, on the Trinity, and the greater context of Scripture and the church. While I was writing, teaching, and preaching, I thought I was working to make a change in my fellowship in the right direction. I figured that I could help in some small way to steer the tradition back to what I now believed to be authentic Christianity. What I was doing, instead, was raising eyebrows and questions among those whom I served. I began finding myself on the defensive. Preaching opportunities began to disappear. I was growing more and more cynical and bitter each day, primarily because I didn't feel that people were willing to make the same sacrifices that I had, and they were not willing to open their eyes and see the things I saw. They did not see the gospel in the same light as me, and, as I wrote before, this was everything to me.

One Sunday in particular, I listened to a preacher completely butcher the gospel story as I now knew it, shredded the Bible as I now understood it, and misrepresent God as I had come to know Him. I remember looking at my wife, and it was if we both understood the same thing at the same moment; this

7. A Final Word?

couldn't continue. I couldn't help people who didn't see there was a problem, and we couldn't continue to be a part of something we no longer believed in and had, in some ways, become spiritually abusive. Even worse, I knew that if I stayed put, I would not be able to teach or preach the same old things I had always been taught, and it would only create dissension and discord. You can call me a lot of things, but I want "church splitter" to never be one of them. But where do you go? How do you find a church that fits you? Is there some sort of an internet quiz?

I say that jokingly, but we found one. My wife and I took it, and it said we were Lutherans. We took it again the next day, and it said we were Anglicans. I still don't know how they calibrated that thing. What I do know is that we spent a lot of time researching faith traditions and learning about traditions other than the ones we knew. We visited other places, met with ministers, and we shared our story with those who would listen. We were looking for a church that understood the Bible not as the final authority to on all matters that needed to be correctly interpreted, but as the primary witness to the truth of Jesus Christ. We were looking for a church that was committed to not only the historic Traditions but also the living presence of Jesus through the Holy Spirit as a guiding presence in the present. We were looking for a group that understood the historic structure of the church and knew its place in that broad spectrum. We were looking for a group that was peculiarly Christian and that when you walked in the church, you knew you it was a Christian house of worship and not a community center or concert venue. We were looking for a church that understood the gospel, the purpose of life, and the place of worship as a means to know God, love God and heal the sin diseased soul. In essence, we were looking for a place that would be formative for our spiritual development and support us in our quest to know the Living God in Jesus Christ. We found all this and more among the Eastern Orthodox Churches with one final twist.

I contacted a local priest, and we began meeting with some regularity. He offered us things to read and questions to consider. I was and am still impressed with his patience and gentle nature. We used to get together and have lunch on occasion and chat about our journey and other related goings-on. There was one such meeting, in particular, that I tossed out a question about converting to Orthodoxy. I'll never forget his response because it changed my perception of all that I had learned thus far. This life-changing response was, "Why?" I thought, "What do you mean, why?" I had imagined that I was an evangelist's dream! I mean, I just asked to jump in his fishing net with little to no work on his part! How could he ask why? Sometimes I wonder if my face showed as much shock as I felt. I responded, "Because I agree with the church theologically, the teachings are sound, and I think it's right on these important issues." To which he replied, "If that's all you've got, then you're not ready. Agreeing with good theology is not enough." I bet my chin hit the floor.

Nevertheless, I thank God for that meeting and his words that day because it sent me searching, yet

7. A Final Word?

again, for something I was missing. What did I lack? Was I like the rich young ruler? Did I need to sell something? What did I need to sell? Better yet, regarding Isaiah 30, was there an idol that needed to be torn down? As I wrote before about identifying one's idols, I had suspected that my idol was rightness itself; perhaps that was the issue? I guess I always had a nagging suspicion that I worshipped the concept of being right, and perhaps I had struggles with all those questions because I couldn't produce a defensible opinion, and they, in some strange way, threatened my ability to worship at the altar of rightness. In a strange twisted way, maybe arguing was my version of witnessing. Perhaps arrogance was my offering, and condemning my opponents was my sick version of veneration. That's when it hit me. There wasn't a maybe or perhaps about it at all. I had an idol that needed to be torn down for sure, and that idol was me.

Here I was, on the one hand, with the churches of Christ trying to make a name for myself because I believed in the rightness of my opinion on all the important issues. Even when I thought I wasn't, I did the work and came up with defensible options that I believed everyone else should subscribe to so that they might be intellectually honest like myself. When that fell apart, I went away on the other hand to a new church saying I'm ready to join up because I think this is right! Yet all along, nothing in me ever really changed, and all my learning had produced no tangible repentance. I was no different in heart, and the only change I was seeking was a change in the labels. Perhaps there was nothing converted about me at all. Perhaps I had found all these new and profound perspectives on faith and had never taken the time to let them change me. In truth, I was too busy being a commentator to be a confessor, and I was too full of rhetoric to repent. He was right. I wasn't ready at all. Sorting through all those personal demons and razing the altars of pride and ambition proved to be some of the most difficult work I ever attempted. The work has begun, but the road ahead is long and demanding. Through this struggle, however, I came across one final perspective that I want to share with you.

Sometimes I think we imagine the whole spectrum of Christianity to be like a big buffet which we go through with our plate picking out the things that agree with our taste. Some go to the buffet and pick contemporary worship music, pastors in skinny jeans and untucked shirts, coffee shops in the foyer, and small groups throughout the week. Others come to the buffet and feel more comfortable with traditional hymns, conservative clothes, hellfire and brimstone preaching, and an "amen" from the back row. Still, others find liturgy appealing, and the smells and bells of the high church truly satisfy their longing. In this model, people could go along mixing and matching new combinations all the time and have a "church experience" that suits them to a T. But in this all too familiar scenario, who or what do you suppose is being worshipped? Is it God, or is it our preferences? Is it the Lord of Creation, or is it the individual? Has worshipping the Lord come down to customization

7. A Final Word?

issues? Perhaps that's what Israel was doing so long ago with her various idols. Are we only looking for our "goldilocks church," the one that fits just right and then defend her honor? How has it come to be like this? I don't ever remember setting out to be like that, but yet, there I was. I had taken my turn at the buffet and turned my nose up at the flavor I had been served all my life and thought I could just simply decide to taste something else that suited me better. Thanks be to God that I was stopped dead in my tracks, for it made me realize that it just can't work like that. Christian faith is not a smorgasbord in which we build our version of Christianity to suit us.

For me, the idol of Isaiah 30 that needed to be torn down was myself, and my sense of rightness. I wanted to be the guy that went to the Christian buffet and selected all the right doctrines and dogmas. As it turns out, doing this causes you to miss everything important; it causes us to miss Jesus. We err when we believe that Jesus is merely a doctrine or a dogma to be rightly interpreted. More than doctrine, He is the living Son of God, and it turns out that you can't worship Him if you're bowing down to the idol of doctrinal rightness. This doesn't mean that we shouldn't care about doctrinal accuracy, far from it. What it means instead is that we love and adore Jesus *more* than our doctrines, and instead of using Jesus as a means to our doctrinal ends, we use our doctrines as a means to find Jesus. Jesus is not a means to an end; rather, he is the whole process from beginning to end. There is a difference in being satisfied with your correct understanding of Jesus and being satisfied with Jesus himself. The former is truth, and the latter is the whole truth.

Idols are hard to tear down when they are your own. It's easy for us to see the idols in other people's life and tear them down by proxy, but it's another thing altogether to rip your idols away from the fabric of self-worth. How do you even find them? What does your life revolve around? To what are you addicted? There is an old illustration that goes something like this. Suppose four people are setting down to dinner, and they are all ordered the same meal. Without looking at their physical appearance, how can you tell which one is the glutton? The glutton, so the story goes, is the one that becomes enraged when the food is delayed or incorrect. The glutton is the one that becomes emotional when the meal is over. The moral of the story is that we need to look for the things in our life that we can't do without. There, we will begin the search for our idols. Naturally, this is easier said than done. The idol worshipper is akin to the addict. Can you imagine how hard it is to lay down an addiction on command? It is never just as easy as refusing the idol or addiction because we have to also deal with a host of different emotions that are tangled up with it. What's even harder to overcome is the idol that has always been there accepting our worship from a young age hiding under the labels of religious piety.

I want to close with a final word to those in the churches of Christ about recognizing the formative power of tradition's current. Like all people raised in a religious context, I was born into a current, and that

7. A Final Word?

current formed me. The current and context of the churches of Christ shaped me and molded me religiously and socially. It set before me what I was to worship and how I was to worship it and called it God. The current made me what I am warts and all, and it released these questions like combatants into the coliseum of my mind. I welcomed the struggle, and I hope you will too because unless we struggle, we will simply drift along. Historically, this doesn't work out too well. If you or someone you know has begun to wrestle with the formative power of tradition in your own life, I want to encourage you to respect the fight and don't quit until you have answers. Have you sought to know who you are really worshipping? Is it the God of Heaven, or is it an imposter idol? God doesn't have grandchildren, so regardless of how we've all been taught, we must all make the ascent to Zion on our own and see for ourselves. We must all set down and take account of how we have been formed historically. From infancy to this moment, we must look at the pattern of our own lives to see how the tradition has cut through the valleys of our identity.

For me, that formative impression from youth to adulthood was the conservative churches of Christ. I know this does not characterize all churches of Christ, but in my experiences, this formative experience was replete with a thirst for rightness at the expense of everyone else. This environment not only instilled a love of being right, but I also picked up a tendency to confuse love with performance, unity with uniformity, and acceptance with agreement. No healthy relationship in the world should work that way, and I think I learned that, and I am still learning that, the hard way. I know I'm not the only one. Sadly, the road diverges here for some.

On the one hand, we could look scornfully at these churches and, filled with bitterness, swear them off forever. Or, on the other hand, we could exemplify the love, unity, and acceptance so scarce in many of those associations. Forgiveness is always the best option, but forgiveness does not mean that we have to continue as if nothing is wrong. Every single faith tradition can be both a scar and solace, and each tradition can be both edifying and destructive. Yet, when they display this evidence of pain and frustration, this should be an indication that something is wrong. Worshipping the light should not produce darkness. I know that all traditions, like people, have skeletons in their closet, and it doesn't always mean that we sink the whole boat because the sail is ripped.

At the same time, however, leaders in the churches of Christ need to realize that many times people are leaving because they are dealing with way more than broken sails. People are leaving in record numbers, and while some leave on poor terms, others leave with valid reasons. I know sometimes people leave because their tastes have changed, and they want to trade in their traditional hymns for contemporary music. Sometimes people leave because of doctrinal issues like women's roles in worship, or sexuality disputes. Those who are leaving for reasons like these are like those at the smorgasbord attempting to find the thing that either suits their taste or ap-

7. A Final Word?

peases their conscience. Hopefully, they'll find what they are after, and their conscience finds peace, but we should remember this; if we are searching for anything but Jesus, we will never be satisfied with what we find. I realize that each church cannot be all things to all people. Fair is fair. I also realize that some people leave because the church environment has become toxic, and they must leave for the health of their family. All these issues are important and need to be addressed continuously by church leadership. At any rate, people are still leaving in record numbers. Many churches of Christ need another great awakening. In some small way, I want to contribute to that much-needed awakening. This is no longer my tradition, but it is filled with close family, friends, and dear loved ones. If it is any solace at all, I want to inform those who lead the churches of Christ today and tomorrow about my "why." I want to alert all who will listen to the reality of the deeper truth that lies beyond the surface layer of truth so commonly mistaken for the sum of it all. The Bible is richer than a 19th century hermeneutic, the church has more texture you could possibly imagine, the gospel is about more than guilt, and life has more implicit meaning than to simply figure out all the rules and follow them.

I pray the next great awakening for the churches of Christ is coming and that it is an awakening not to new doctrinal awareness but to the awareness of light and life in Jesus himself. I pray that churches of Christ can find a fresh appreciation for the Bible not as a pattern for life but as a witness to Life. I pray that they'll move to appreciate the whole truth, not just part of it. I pray that the church begins to recognize the Church not as something that needs to be restored but as a group of humans in need of repentance. I pray that they'll find authentic and meaningful ways to bear the Image of Christ, be the Image of Christ, and live the gospel message in its fullness. I pray that the RM becomes a movement focused not on restoring what they believe to be ancient Christianity but on restoring the life lost in Eden to all humanity. In the grand scheme of things, the RM is still very young. Time will tell how this tradition will survive, thrive, and continue to form new generations of disciples. For me, however, I know that I am too broken to help repair it. I suspect many more will come to that same conclusion. I pray these reflections help all who read them to find the fullness of life in Christ. If that is in the churches of Christ, thanks be to God. If it isn't, may God lead your search into His loving arms. What we can all be sure of, however, is that Jesus is bigger than any movement and following Jesus is a Tradition in and of itself. If we are to live, and I mean truly live, we will have to trade the very blood in our veins for His, and with Paul, we will have to confess:

> *"I am crucified with Christ: nevertheless I live; yet not I, but Christ liveth in me: and the life which I now live in the flesh I live by the faith of the Son of God, who loved me, and gave himself for me. I do not frustrate the grace of God: for if righteousness come by the law, then Christ is dead in vain."* (Gal. 2:20, KJV)

To God be the glory in all things.

About the Cover

The icon on the front cover features St. Symeon, known in the Orthodox Church as the God-Receiver. He gets this title because he received the Divine Child, God enfleshed, in his arms when Mary and Joseph brought him to the Temple 40 days after his birth, as was the custom according to the law. The story is recorded in Luke 2:25-35. By an unknown Russian Iconographer, this version accents Symeon's gaze as he beholds the living "restoration of Israel." I chose an icon of St. Symeon the God-Receiver for several reasons.

First, in the Orthodox Liturgical Calendar, St. Symeon is commemorated along with the Prophetess Anna the day after we remember the Presentation of our Lord in the Temple. The Presentation of our Lord, or Meeting of the Lord as it is sometimes called, is the feast day of the Church on which my wife and I were received into the Orthodox Church. It is a fitting day on which to receive the Lord as it is the day we commemorate the Lord Himself being received into the arms of a righteous and hopeful soul so many years ago. In that way, St. Symeon symbolizes my journey.

Second, as tradition goes, St. Symeon was a man well advanced in years. The Church's tradition passes on that he was one of the Septuagint translators several hundred years before Christ. As he was translating a passage from the prophet Isaiah (7:14 – behold a virgin shall conceive and bear a son), an angel appeared to him and told him that he wouldn't die until he saw that very thing happen. And so, as the story goes, he was 360 years old when he received the infant Jesus in his arms. He waited a substantially long time just to lay his eyes on the Lord's salvation and the "light of the gentiles." Although not as long as St. Symeon, I too waited and struggled for many years, longing to see "salvation" and the "glory of Israel." In that way, St. Symeon symbolizes my journey.

Lastly, the Church has never forgotten the words of St. Symeon. One such example comes from the Vespers service where, near the end, the Priest exclaims the words of St. Symeon saying, "Lord, now let thou thy servant depart in peace, according to thy word; for mine eyes have seen thy salvation which thou hast prepared in the presence of all peoples, a light for revelation to the Gentiles, and for glory to thy people Israel."[74] These words echo my sentiment concerning the churches of Christ – "Lord, now let thy servant depart in peace, according to thy word; for mine eyes have seen thy salvation." I've never wished to leave the tradition of my youth on bad terms; I never wished to split congregations, sow discord among brethren, or lay stumbling blocks in the paths of little ones. I pray for peace. Nevertheless, when Mary puts the Son of God in your arms, your perspective changes. In this way, St. Symeon symbolizes my journey.

For these reasons, the icon of St. Symeon the God-Receiver is the icon of my journey and this book. Now this book is in your hands like the Son of God was in the hands of the Righteous Symeon. Behold,

---

[74] Luke 2:29-32

About the Author

even now St. Symeon says, "This child is destined for the falling and the rising of many in Israel, and to be a sign that will be opposed so that the inner thoughts of many will be revealed..."[75]

Icon used by permission courtesy of Uncut Mountain Supply. This Icon, and many others, available at www.uncutmountainsupply.com.

---

[75] Luke 2:34–35

About the Author

Andrew Burns began preaching for the churches of Christ in southern West Virginia at the age of 16. Following in the footsteps of his childhood preacher, he became a teacher to support himself and help small congregations across the state who could not afford a full-time preacher. After 20 years of dealing with tragedy and trauma, Andrew began to have more questions than answers. He obtained a Master's degree in Christian Ministry from Abilene Christian University and began searching with more intention than before. His quest led him to the Greek Orthodox Church, which Andrew and his wife now call home. They were received into the faith in February of 2020. Today, Andrew Burns is beginning to know Christ more thoroughly than ever before, and he longs for all of the brothers and sisters in his previous tradition to experience the abundant life he has found.

If you enjoyed this book, please consider leaving an online review on Amazon, Apple Book store, or other retailer. The author would appreciate reading your thoughts.

About the Publisher

Sulis International Press publishes select fiction and nonfiction in a variety of genres under four imprints: Riversong Books, Sulis Academic Press, Sulis Press, and Keledei Publications.

For more, visit the website at

https://sulisinternational.com
Subscribe to the newsletter at
https://sulisinternational.com/subscribe/

Follow on social media
https://www.facebook.com/SulisInternational
https://twitter.com/Sulis_Intl
https://www.pinterest.com/Sulis_Intl/
https://www.instagram.com/sulis_international/

www.ingramcontent.com/pod-product-compliance
Lightning Source LLC
Chambersburg PA
CBHW030151100526
44592CB00009B/226